HAUNTING POE

HAUNTING POE

His Afterlife in Richmond & Beyond

Christopher P. Semtner

THE
History
PRESS

Published by The History Press
Charleston, SC
www.historypress.com

Copyright © 2022 by Christopher P. Semtner
All rights reserved

Cover art by Chris Semtner.
All other images courtesy of the Poe Museum.

First published 2022

Manufactured in the United States

ISBN 9781467151269

Library of Congress Control Number: 2021952402

CONTENTS

ACKNOWLEDGEMENTS

The following work was made possible by the generosity of several different people and entities too numerous to mention. Thanks are due to Laura Hoff, library and Edgar Cayce Foundation manager at Edgar Cayce's Association of Research and Enlightenment, for allowing me access to their collection of Andrew Jackson Davis books and correspondence during my research. Susan Jaffe Tane provided the travel grant that allowed me to attend the International Poe & Hawthorne Conference in Kyoto, where I presented the paper about Poe and Spiritualism that eventually led to this book. The Edgar Allan Poe Museum's reference library and archives have also been a valuable resource well before this book was ever conceived. I would also like to thank Jeb, Smokey, Jack, Pumpkin, Patchy, Edgar and Pluto for their support.

INTRODUCTION

A ghost told me to write this book. Sort of.
During a paranormal investigation of the Edgar Allan Poe Museum some years ago, a psychic medium announced that he was receiving a message for me from Poe's wife. It must have been about midnight one frigid winter evening. The museum and grounds were dark except for the flickering blue glow of a few video cameras' LED screens. All was silent, save for the howls and laughter of drunken revelers stumbling down Main Street from one bar to the next.

The medium, who had traveled the world to speak with spirits, publishing several books on his experiences along the way, nearly whispered, "Poe's wife Elizabeth wants me to tell you something."

"Do you mean Virginia?" I asked. That was his wife's name, after all.

"Oh, yes," the psychic said. "She has a message for you."

Considering that she has been dead since 1847, long before my parents' parents' parents were born, I was curious what Virginia Poe might have to say to me.

He continued, "Elizabeth says you should write the book, the one you were thinking about. She says you should do it."

While that medium might have lost a little credibility by forgetting Virginia's name twice in a row, he did inspire me to write another book.

This medium was not the first to search the museum for earthbound spirits. Paranormal investigators have prowled the garden after hours with video cameras and electromagnetic field detectors while guided ghost tours gather in the parking lot in hopes of seeing a face peering back at them from the window of a supposedly vacant room. Occasional museum guests have been known to inform their tour guides that a specter is standing behind them. One of the older guides even told me she had been hit in the back of the head by a nail from an empty corner of a room during one of her guided tours.

It seems that people either *expect* the museum to be a hotbed of paranormal activity or simply wish it were, and I am not about to settle that matter. I suppose those who ask if the Poe Museum is haunted do not want to hear about the legend of the little boy in colonial-era clothing who plays in the garden or the elderly lady who extends a warm welcome to visitors in the gift shop. (I have not seen either of them myself.) Rather, they want to know if Edgar Allan Poe is still hanging around, just about to give someone a good scare.

After all, he wrote some great thrillers about ladies with names like Ligeia, Morella and Eleonora who refuse to cross over to the other side. The title character in "Ligeia" believes that her will is strong enough to conquer death, and she eventually returns to take control of her widower's second wife's body. In "Morella," the title character dies in childbirth while threatening to return by occupying her newborn daughter's body. Eleonora, from the story of that name, crosses over from the spirit world to ensure her earthbound widower remains true to his promise to stay faithful to her after her death.

Then there is the mysterious shade in his tale "Shadow—A Fable," who comes to claim the survivors of an ancient epidemic. "The Masque of the Red Death" presents a party crasher dressed in a bloody shroud and skull mask. When the guests tear off his costume, they find nothing underneath. That is when the revelers contract the dreaded plague known as the Red Death. "MS Found in a Bottle" features a whole ship full of ghosts, doomed to sail the seas for eternity.

His tales "The Colloquy of Monos and Una," "The Conversation of Eiros and Charmion" and "The Power of Words" are presented in the form of dialogues between spirits in the afterlife. As such, they explore themes of death, eternity and the hereafter.

The many appearances of these concepts in Poe's works suggest both his personal interest in the great mysteries of life after death and the public's shared interest in these enigmas. He lived in an age when his readers were primed to ask such questions and to search for answers not only in church but also at the séance table.

Edgar Allan Poe from a daguerreotype taken in Providence in 1848.

Before we begin, it might be helpful to provide a brief outline of the poet's life. Born in Boston in 1809, the same year that Abraham Lincoln and Charles Darwin were born, Poe was orphaned in Richmond two years later and taken in by the childless John and Frances Allan, who fostered him. He studied in London and Richmond before attending the University of Virginia in 1826, the year its founder, Thomas Jefferson, died. Without sufficient funds to pay his tuition, Poe dropped out of college after his first year and enlisted in the army for two years. After his foster mother's death, he attended the United States Military Academy at West Point but got himself expelled in 1831, after just eight months. Shortly after his expulsion, he published his third slim volume of poetry, which included early versions of "The Sleeper," "Lenore," "Al Aaraaf" and other poems exploring different aspects of death, mourning and the afterlife. Of course, writing poetry about the death of a loved one was not at all unusual in those days of prolonged and increasingly regimented mourning customs. Poe's contemporaries perfected the art of grieving.

Moving to Baltimore, he began writing fiction for the magazine market, eventually winning a short story contest and accepting an editorial position at a magazine back in Richmond. While there, he married his cousin, Virginia Clemm, in 1836, the year before Queen Victoria married Prince Albert. The search for more lucrative magazine work soon took him to New York, Philadelphia and New York again. His fame grew steadily with the publication of his first detective tales (a genre he invented forty-six years before Arthur Conan Doyle published the first Sherlock Holmes mystery) and his hoaxes, but the appearance of his poem "The Raven" in 1845 made the thirty-six-year-old poet a household name. He would not, however, have much time to enjoy his fame. His wife died two years later, and he followed her another two years after that, in 1849. His last book, *Eureka*, was Poe's attempt to solve all the mysteries of life, death and the universe. Among the few possessions he left behind was his personal copy filled with notes to be included in an expanded second edition that he never lived to see.

His life coincided with the rapid expansion of new technologies for communication, transportation and medicine existing alongside a boom in pseudosciences, quack remedies and outright hoaxes. New Protestant sects arrived just as quickly as entirely new religions influenced by the beliefs from distant cultures came to the scene. This was an age of exploration and experimentation, when every new discovery or development promised the hope of a cure, technology or solution that would have seemed impossible a couple decades earlier.

As a magazine editor, Poe was right in the middle of it all. His fiction appeared alongside reports of the newest inventions and experiments, and it was becoming increasingly difficult to tell the facts from the fiction. After his death, the problem only got worse. Rumors began to spread about attempts to contact Poe's ghost. Some were even believed to have succeeded. Stories were also told about Poe's spirit making appearances in order to guide, to communicate or simply to frighten the living. What follows are some of those accounts.

We will start by introducing you to Poe's world, its supernatural beliefs and its quest for spiritual knowledge. Then we will examine Poe's place within and outside the mysticism of his time. Finally, we will recount some of the many ghostly legends associated with Poe himself.

Let me begin with the opening sentence of Poe's tale "The Black Cat": "For the most wild, yet most homely narrative which I am about to pen, I neither expect nor solicit belief."

part i

POE'S HAUNTED CHILDHOOD

The spirits of the dead who stood
In life before thee are again
In death around thee—and their will
Shall overshadow thee: be still.

—Edgar Allan Poe, "Spirits of the Dead"

Chapter 1

SUMMONING THE SPIRITS

It was one of those muggy summer afternoons in the Shenandoah Valley of western Virginia. The curly-haired five-year-old future poet was riding on the back of the saddle with his uncle Edward Valentine, who used to take the boy out riding with him to pick up the mail in Staunton, an old trading post turned city nestled between the Blue Ridge and Allegheny Mountains. Little Edgar was a sensitive child with large, dark eyes. He displayed a devotion to his foster mother and a fondness for animals, especially his pet cat, Tib.

Valentine took advantage of these post office visits to pick up a newspaper and, handing it to Edgar, would ask him to read it aloud to the locals, who were astounded by the boy's precocity. Other times, Valentine challenged local children to box with Edgar, who invariably won.

This particular day, on the way back from the post office, Valentine's horse passed an overgrown country cemetery behind a log cabin. Edgar screamed, and Valentine clutched the struggling boy to keep him from jumping off the horse and running the other way. When Valentine refused to loosen his grip, Edgar pleaded, tears streaming down his face, "They will run after us and drag me down!" The boy would not stop kicking and swinging until the graves were well out of sight.

Only after they returned to Valentine's farm did Poe explain that the elderly enslaved woman who had cared for him for the Allans back in Richmond used to take him downstairs to the servants' quarters at night to tell him stories of ghosts and graveyards.

The burying grounds at Richmond's St. John's Church in 1890.

From an early age, Poe was a devotee of such African American folk tales. Even as an adult, he enjoyed meeting with Black people, both free and enslaved, who shared their tales with him. While on a visit to the Brunswick County plantation of his college friend Thomas Goode Tucker, Poe avoided playing field sports or socializing with his fellow guests, according to a 1916 account recorded by his host's nephew. The poet spent most his visit alone in his bedroom, writing. Aside from solving math puzzles with his host, the only thing Poe seemed to enjoy was meeting an enslaved man named Armistead, who lived at a nearby plantation with his African-born wife. Sitting together in Armistead's cabin, they told the writer lurid tales of ghosts, African magic and Hoodoo. Fascinated by these stories, Poe declared Armistead to be the most interesting man he had ever met.

But just what tales did Armistead tell him? So many of these folk traditions were passed down orally for generations before being written down that it is difficult to know precisely which ones Poe might have heard. Poe scholar Thomas Ollive Mabbott believed the Afro-Caribbean tradition of the Evil Eye might have inspired him to write in "The Tell-Tale Heart" about an otherwise harmless old man whose "vulture eye" drives his companion to madness and murder.

Poe's tale "The Black Cat," in which a black cat's screams reveal a murderer's crime, could also be influenced by folk tales like one recorded in

Wise County, Virginia, by James Taylor Adams in 1941. In the version of the oral tradition that Adams recorded, a mother secretly kills her children and convinces everyone that they died of natural causes. She almost gets away with the crime until a large black cat appears before her. It "squalled and walked to the bed and reared up on it and looked the sick woman square in the face." In response, the murderer "screamed out that it was the devil come to get her for killing her children" and dropped dead on the spot. This folk tale contains motifs—including the giant black cat, the cat's luminous eyes and the black cat being the devil in disguise—found in numerous such traditions originating from both European and African traditions, so it is impossible to know just which ones inspired Poe's short story or precisely how much of a debt his terror tales owe to the stories he heard from the Allans' servants or Armistead.

Through his relations with African Americans, Poe could also have learned about Hoodoo, the secretive belief system practiced by enslaved Africans in North America. Adherents might practice divining the future from dreams, the stars or omens; cursing enemies; or conjuring the spirits of the dead.

Thirty miles south of the Allan home, businessman Charles O'Hara of Petersburg, Virginia, depended on his Afro-Caribbean slave for advice in warding off evil spirits. The latter informed him that ghosts could only occupy homes with right angles, so naturally, O'Hara built his new home with absolutely no right angles. That home, known as Trapezium House, was constructed in 1817 and is still standing on Market Street as a reminder of the latent influence of Hoodoo, fortunetellers and diviners of signs and omens on Poe's Virginia.

Southeast of Richmond, in Southampton County, an enslaved man named Nat Turner used augury, or the reading of omens, to determine when he should launch a rebellion against his master. Interpreting an 1831 eclipse as a sign that the time had arrived to revolt, Turner and his men killed about sixty people, and the militia, in turn, killed twice as many of them, including Turner. History remembers the event as Turner's Rebellion. Poe was twenty-two at the time, living in Baltimore.

Another means of divination was the walking boy. In practice, the conjurer would place a beetle inside a bottle. Whichever way the insect walked, the person pulled the bottle in the same direction with a string. Using this method, one could find a hidden spell bottle or locate one's enemy. The tradition sounds somewhat reminiscent of Poe's tale "The Gold-Bug," in which the titular insect, tied to a string and lowered through a skull's eye, is used to help find a treasure.

Conjurers could summon spirits of the dead to kill, to cure disease or to help find lost money. The soil from a grave, which possessed the power of the dead reposing beneath it, could be kept in a small sack for magical purposes. Such tales of the powers ascribed to graves and grave soil might have inspired the young Edgar's attempt to flee from the old cemetery in Staunton.

Ghosts were not confined to cemeteries, either. One of Poe's contemporaries, the Virginia planter Edmund Ruffin, recorded the accounts of the slaves he met on a trip to South Carolina. One of them recalled seeing a spirit running around a fountain, while another claimed to have seen a ghost sitting on a plank.

The budding writer would also have heard numerous other ghost stories during his early years in Richmond. There is even a legend surrounding the daughter of the city's founder, William Byrd II. After her father forbade her to marry the Englishman she loved, Evelyn Byrd supposedly pined away for him until she died at an early age. (Pining away over a lost love was apparently a legitimate cause of death at the time.) Thereafter, her spirit returned to visit her friend at a nearby plantation. Supposedly, Evelyn's specter can still be glimpsed floating among the tall boxwoods at Westover, her father's James River plantation.

When Poe was six, his foster parents took him with them for a five-year stay in Scotland and England. While in Irvine, Scotland, Poe lived with John Allan's sister in Bridgegate House and, according to Robert Brill's *The Mystery of "Mar'se Eddie" in the Shire*, took frequent walks in nearby Lord Kilmarnock's Park, "where the ghost of a lady was rumored to be seen sometimes." Between the legends he might have heard in Scotland and the gothic tales he certainly read in *Blackwood's Edinburgh Magazine* upon his return to Richmond, the young writer had no shortage of inspiration for his own supernatural tales. His first published short story, "Metzengerstein," was just such a European-style gothic piece, complete with the requisite haunted castle, family curse and horrifying finale.

Poe's was an age abounding with ghost stories, dark omens and supernatural tales. Before modern science and technology brought light to the darkness, the night was a dangerous and mysterious place. It is no wonder the future horror writer might have grown up feeling surrounded by the supernatural. As recorded in Susan Weiss's *The Home Life of Poe*, one of Poe's closest childhood friends recalled the young Poe's greatest fear:

> *Mr. John Mackenzie, in speaking of Edgar, bore witness to his high spirit and pluckiness in occasional schoolboy encounters, and also to his timidity in*

regard to being alone at night and his belief in and fear of the supernatural. He had heard Poe say, when grown, that the most horrible thing he could imagine as a boy was to feel an ice-cold hand laid upon his face in a pitch-dark room when alone at night; or to awaken in semi-darkness and see an evil face gazing close into his own; and that these fancies had so haunted him that he would often keep his head under the bed-covering until nearly suffocated.

Although there is no way to enumerate every ghost story Poe might have heard, what follows are a few supernatural occurrences that likely impacted his early years.

Chapter 2

THE THEATER FIRE

The dashing young naval lieutenant James Gibbon had battled pirates in Tripoli, been imprisoned by slave traders in North Africa and returned home to Richmond a hero. He had stared down death too many times to count. But *this* vision chilled him to the core. Never had a sight so repulsed him, even if he did not know why—even if it was only a dream.

When Gibbon rose one morning, he barely touched his breakfast. It was the day after Christmas 1811, and he was planning on escorting his sweetheart, Sallie Conyers, to the Richmond Theater that evening. Although he had every reason to be happy, he could not shake that nightmare from his mind.

Noticing the change that had come over him since the previous day, his sister asked him why he seemed so melancholy. As she recorded in her diary, he answered:

> *You all laugh at me I know, but I have had such a horrible dream that it has depressed me. I dreamt I was standing before a closed door about to enter, but conscious of some nameless horror something told me to keep back. The door slowly opened and I went in and found myself in a large hall dark and empty. After a few steps I saw a man's face standing out of the darkness, illuminated by a lurid light. All else was dark, the man's eyes were fixed on me and I was seized with a horror and depression I could not shake off.*

From the front window of his parents' house, he could make out the brick mansion looming over the lot across the street. Everybody called it Moldavia after Molly and David Randolph, who used to live there. The

Randolphs were one of the wealthiest families in Virginia and boasted presidents, senators, judges and the like among their relatives. A few years earlier, David Randolph lost the house, and a merchant—and immigrant— Joseph Gallego, bought the place. He and his wife, Mary, had since taken in the young Sallie Conyers.

Conyers was twenty and reputedly very pretty with a long neck, abundant curls and classical features. Gibbon planned to marry her one day.

But his vision of impending danger could not be ignored. As much as he hated to disappoint her, Gibbon needed to convince her not to attend the theater that evening. His pleas went unheard.

A FEW BLOCKS NORTHEAST of the Gibbon house, in a broad double house on Leigh Street, Nancy Green was also anxious about attending the theater that night to see her mother perform the role of the Bleeding Nun in the pantomime of the same name. The ward of Patrick and Eleanor Gibson, Nancy was eager to celebrate her sixteenth birthday the next day, but she refused to go to the theater. Eleanor informed her that she did not have any choice in the matter. Nancy would join her foster family that night, whether she liked it or not.

What happened next was recorded in an unpublished 1922 manuscript now housed in the Virginia Historical Society. The author, Nannie Dunlop Werth, heard the story from her grandmother Ann Dent Hayes McRae, who had also attended the play that night. According to Werth's account, the afternoon after her argument about attending the theater, Nancy decided to walk into town on an errand. While crossing a ravine at Eighth Street, she heard a ghostly voice chant, "Nancy, Nancy, Nancy Green, you'll die before you are sixteen."

She fled home to beg Mrs. Gibson for permission to stay home that night. Werth's grandmother witnessed the exchange. She must not have put much stock in this ghost story because she joined Nancy and Eleanor that evening.

Even aside from Gibbon's and Green's premonitions, the city was already on edge after a year of dark omens including tornados, volcanic eruptions, a comet and the New Madrid earthquake that nearly toppled Richmond's homes and businesses. A sense of impending doom was in the air. A Richmonder of the time, Thomas Brown, wrote in his diary:

> *This was a winter of fear and trembling, especially with the superstitious and weak minded. A large comet had appeared in the fall accompanied*

by a long season of warm dry and sultry weather, and many speculations were made in the paper about it, some contending that it was approaching the earth and might come near enough to destroy it. There were some severe shocks of earthquakes, the severest ever experienced in Virginia. In Richmond some houses rocked and chimneys fell.... To complete the whole, a crazy man or a knave, wrote a prophecy published in pamphlets that the world would be destroyed on a certain day and many believed it. Some actually died of imagination and fear.

Back at Moldavia, Mary Gallego received word that a family emergency would prevent her friend Jane Scott Mackenzie from joining her and Sallie to see the play. A couple weeks earlier, Mackenzie had taken in the daughter of one of the other actresses who had been performing at the Richmond Theater. This actress, Eliza Poe, had recently succumbed to tuberculosis, leaving her daughter, Rosalie, and sons, Henry and Edgar, orphans. As you know, Edgar went to live with the Allans, who soon left town to celebrate the Christmas season with friends on nearby Turkey Island. The Mackenzies, however, remained in Richmond, and Mrs. Mackenzie planned to go to the theater with Mary Gallego. At least, she *had* planned to go before one of her children, possibly Rosalie Poe, got sick. Staying home to care for that child probably saved her life.

Gibbon's mother and sister called at Moldavia while Sallie was still dressing. Ever since James had informed her of his refusal to see the play, she no longer wanted to go. She reluctantly prepared for the show while grilling James's sister for details about his strange behavior. When Mrs. Gallego complained that Sallie's necklace did not match her dress, Miss Gibbon lent her one of her own.

Just after sunset, Mary and Sallie took the short ride uphill to the Richmond Theater. The long wooden building stood at the summit of a steep hill, no more than a block from the gallows that loomed over the edge where the plateau plunges into Shockoe Valley. The structure was about ninety feet long, fifty feet wide and three stories tall. A semicircular bull's-eye window peaked out from one of the gable ends. Far below that eye was the main entrance, through which Gallego and Conyers entered.

The doors opened onto a dark lobby where the women might have seen other theatergoers, including Virginia's governor, George Smith, and other prominent politicians, in addition to wealthy influencers like Eleanor Gibson, Ann McRae and Nancy Green. While the average citizens scrambled to find seats on the first floor, Gallego, Conyers and Gibson ascended the narrow staircase, which creaked and swayed as they made their way to the private boxes upstairs. The stairs and boxes were supported by tall wooden posts that groaned under the weight of their occupants.

From Gallego's box, Conyers could see the stage on one side and the gallery seating for the poor, prostitutes, slaves and freedmen on the opposite end. Overhead, painted canvas was spread over the horizontal beams that crossed the bare pine ceiling. Beneath her, she could see the room packed to capacity. Somehow, the management had managed to squeeze nearly six hundred people in there.

In a nearby box, she caught sight of James Gibbon, returning her gaze. Exchanging smiles, they settled into their seats for the night's first musical number. Against his better judgement, Gibbon had come to the theater, though he could not shake the suffocating sense that he was doomed.

By the time the entertainment began at seven o'clock, the room's only light was coming from the chandeliers. The crowd had gathered for five hours of performances to include four musical numbers and two plays, Denis Diderot's *The Father; or, Family Feuds* and Matthew Lewis's *Raymond and Agnes; or, the Bleeding Nun*. It was during the latter that Gibbon saw the face. The menacing figure from his nightmare was suddenly before him, performing on the stage. During the intermission, Gibbon hurried outside to calm his nerves. He was crossing Capitol Square, under the shadow of Thomas Jefferson's Neoclassical state capitol, the cold, fresh air biting at his nose, when he heard the screams.

Back in the theater, a stagehand noticed that one of the backstage chandeliers had been raised with two candles still burning, but when he tried to lower the chandelier, it got stuck and started swinging. One of the flames grazed a canvas backdrop, setting it ablaze. The patrons did not stand a chance. Fire engulfed the wooden building and its canvas ceiling and props before the actor had a chance to shout a warning from the stage. The staircase collapsed under the weight of the patrons evacuating the box seats. People downstairs piled against the main entrance, which blocked their escape because it opened inward. The only hope for survival was jumping out the window, which Ann McRae did. She fell two stories to be caught by a man outside.

Nancy's mother, who had been performing just before the fire, ran out the back door to search for her daughter among the evacuees. She never found her. Nancy did not live to be sixteen.

Gibbon arrived in time to see flames blasting through the bull's-eye window as if the building had transformed into a giant fire-breathing dragon.

The Richmond Theater Fire depicted in an 1812 lithograph by B. Tanner.

Pushing through the heaps of dead and wounded escapees, he broke into the theater and managed to find his beloved Sallie among the thick smoke, falling embers and agonized wails. He was last seen carrying her limp body to the exit. Their charred remains were later uncovered locked in an embrace. His family recognized his navy buttons and her borrowed necklace. Mary Gallego's ashes were only identifiable by her jewelry. All that remained of the governor was a "crisped heap."

The building was gone within an hour. Seventy-two people had perished. An unknown number were injured. The city went into deepest mourning, banning theatrical performances for months. Newspapers across the country carried reports of this almost inconceivable tragedy. Some papers deemed the fire God's just wrath against the sinful profession of acting.

John Marshall, the chief justice of the United States Supreme Court, headed the committee tasked with memorializing the fire's victims. The group decided to leave the victims there, burying the charred bones and ashes in two large boxes in the old orchestra pit. Above their crypt was built a church, itself designed to resemble an ancient tomb.

Poe's foster father, John Allan, was one of the new Monumental Church's founding members and purchased pew number eighty. It was here that the young Poe worshipped with his foster mother. He could not have helped noticing the symbols of death and mourning that decorate the building. He certainly would have understood the reason why the parishioners entered through the side entrances each Sunday and why the front door was only opened on Easter. He surely saw Mary Gallego's portrait hanging in his sister's house since Joseph Gallego gave it to Jane Scott Mackenzie. In gratitude for his support, Mackenzie named one of her daughters Mary Gallego Mackenzie and one of her sons Joseph Gallego Mackenzie. The Poe Museum now owns both Mary Gallego's portrait and a painting of Jane Scott Mackenzie in which she wears a locket bearing the letters "J.G."

Poe knew about the fire and the scars it left on his hometown, but did he know the story of Nancy Green's ghostly warning? Even though the version recounted here descended directly from a witness and survivor of the fire, Mary Wingfield Scott's 1951 book *Houses of Old Richmond* contains two other versions. One attributes the lines of the ominous chant to a fortuneteller, and the other places them in a dream from the night before the tragedy. If Poe did not hear the original version, he could have known either of these.

A few years after the fire, when Poe moved with his foster parents into Moldavia, would he have heard about James Gibbon's premonition?

Accounts like these of spiritual visitors appearing to warn or assist the living are among the kinds of ghost stories he would have been familiar with. An acquaintance of Poe's recounted that, although the poet did not know anything about the new Spiritualist movement, Poe did believe in "helper spirits." Virginia folk tales and ghost stories abound with such beings who are said to help the living avoid danger or find hidden money. Poe's own tales do not necessarily feature such spirits, unless we include "Eleonora," whose kind spirit gives her widower permission to remarry after he defies her dying wish by finding a new love.

Gibbon's and Green's stories also reflect Poe's contemporaries' keen awareness of stars, signs and omens. The young Poe watched the stars through his telescope from Moldavia's second-floor porch. As he studied both astronomy and astrology, his mature poetry sometimes incorporates the symbolism of stars and omens. "The Evening Star" and "Ulalume" are probably the best examples.

Memories and legends of the Richmond Theater Fire may also have played some small part in inspiring one of his greatest poems. Set in a theater, "The Conqueror Worm" ends with the actors being consumed by a blood-red worm.

LO! 'tis a gala night
  Within the lonesome latter years!
An angel throng, bewinged, bedight
  In veils, and drowned in tears,
Sit in a theatre, to see
  A play of hopes and fears,
While the orchestra breathes fitfully
  The music of the spheres.

Mimes, in the form of God on high,
  Mutter and mumble low,
And hither and thither fly—
  Mere puppets they, who come and go
At bidding of vast formless things
  That shift the scenery to and fro,
Flapping from out their Condor wings
  Invisible Wo!

That motley drama—oh, be sure
  It shall not be forgot!
With its Phantom chased for evermore,
  By a crowd that seize it not,
Through a circle that ever returneth in
  To the self-same spot,
And much of Madness, and more of Sin,
  And Horror the soul of the plot.

But see, amid the mimic rout
  A crawling shape intrude!
A blood-red thing that writhes from out
  The scenic solitude!
It writhes!—it writhes!—with mortal pangs
  The mimes become its food,
And seraphs sob at vermin fangs
  In human gore imbued.

Out—out are the lights—out all!
  And, over each quivering form,
The curtain, a funeral pall,

Monumental Church from an engraving printed around 1812.

Comes down with the rush of a storm,
While the angels, all pallid and wan,
Uprising, unveiling, affirm
That the play is the tragedy, "Man,"
And its hero the Conqueror Worm.

In Monumental Church, pew number eighty still bears the bronze plaque installed there in 1829 in memory of Poe's foster mother. Those lucky enough to join one of the Historic Richmond Foundation's occasional tours of the site can sit in Poe's seat and almost hear the echo of the old-time hymns they sang so long ago.

The church lost its congregation over half a century ago, so most of the time the building lies silent and empty. Underneath the sanctuary, a dirt-floored crypt contains a brick vault enclosing all that remains of James Gibbon, Sallie Conyers, Nancy Green and sixty-nine other victims of Richmond's first great tragedy.

Chapter 3

THE LADY OF THE LAKE

A t the age of eighteen, Poe published a slim volume of the poetry
he had written in his youth. The printer issued only a few dozen
copies, and they were not distributed. Poe never even owned a
copy. One of the poems from this, his first book, *Tamerlane and Minor Poems*,
was titled "The Lake." After revising it several times over his career, he
released this final version:

In spring of youth it was my lot
To haunt of the wide earth a spot
The which I could not love the less—
So lovely was the loneliness
Of a wild lake, with black rock bound,
And the tall pines that towered around.

But when the Night had thrown her pall
Upon that spot, as upon all,
And the mystic wind went by
Murmuring in melody—
Then—ah then I would awake
To the terror of the lone lake.

Yet that terror was not fright,
But a tremulous delight—

A feeling not the jewelled mine
Could teach or bribe me to define—
Nor Love—although the Love were thine.

Death was in that poisonous wave,
And in its gulf a fitting grave
For him who thence could solace bring
To his lone imagining—
Whose solitary soul could make
An Eden of that dim lake.

When Poe wrote about that "dim lake," there were only two natural lakes in Virginia. One, far out west in the mountains, Poe probably never saw, but he likely visited the other one. And it seems to fit the poem's description much better.

To this day, it is isolated not so much by distance as by time. The place exists in some distant epoch ruled by snakes and slithering things and to which humans are intruders. Accessible by a canal that lurches through the forbidding mass of cypresses, vines, bears, bobcats and reptiles, the lake was long a hiding place for pirates and outlaws. George Washington despised the place so much that he tried to drain the wetlands to erase their stain from the earth forever.

When William Byrd II, the founder of Richmond, explored the area while mapping Virginia's southern border, he found it such a Godforsaken wasteland that he named it the Great Dismal Swamp. At its heart, enclosed by millions of acres of tangled vegetation, is Lake Drummond, with its tea-colored water enshrouded in morning fog and swimming with water moccasins and, at one point, alligators.

By Poe's time, runaway slaves were finding refuge in the swamp's dark recesses, where even the slave catchers dared not pursue them. There, they built settlements where they could live off the abundant wildlife and work for free Black people.

During Poe's childhood, tourists could take a flatboat down the canal to a hotel on the line between Virginia and North Carolina. This was the perfect place for romantic getaways or to drink of brown water, which was already noted for its antibacterial qualities. In those days before refrigeration, sailors found that they could carry barrels of it across the Atlantic without it going bad. No less a dignitary than President James Monroe visited those enchanted waters when Poe was nine years old.

As expected, the hotel also had a lawless side. Its position between jurisdictions attracted duelists. Though the practice was outlawed in 1810, in Virginia, when an offense to one's honor must be satisfied, dueling grounds could be found tucked away on the outskirts of many a town well into the 1880s. Gamblers in the hotel itself could move to the North Carolina side of the hotel if Virginia law enforcement showed up and then push their tables back to the Virginia side of the room as needed.

Poe could have traveled the canal to see Lake Drummond with the Allans, and he certainly would have seen paintings and engravings of the lake by the Virginia artist John Gadsby Chapman. In fact, when the thirty-one-year-old Poe wrote an article about interior design titled "The Philosophy of Furniture" for the May 1840 issue of *Burton's Magazine*, he recommended that a tastefully decorated room should contain a print of Chapman's painting *The Lake of the Great Dismal Swamp*.

By the time Poe would have visited Lake Drummond, the Irish poet Thomas Moore, who toured the lake in 1803, had published "A Ballad: The Lake of the Dismal Swamp," a poem inspired by one of the place's ghostly legends, that of a Native American bride who died just before her intended wedding day. Her glowing figure was doomed to paddle the lake at night in a white canoe, her path lit by a firefly lantern. Overcome

The Lake of the Dismal Swamp engraved in 1829 after a painting by Henry Inman.

by grief, her bereaved lover eventually followed her into the lake, never to return.

After hearing the story in a Norfolk, Virginia tavern, Moore decided to see the swamp for himself. His guide, by the way, had never heard the legend, which Moore's poem would soon make famous throughout the English-speaking world. The poem's celebrity sparked a boom in Dismal Swamp tourism in the early nineteenth century, about the time Poe would have visited. After sunset, tourists scanned the waters for signs of the luminous bride, and a few actually claimed to catch of glimpse of her light flitting about on the water.

Could Poe and the Allans have witnessed her forlorn spirit? Poe scholar Thomas Ollive Mabbott believed that Poe's poem "The Lake," which references this ghost story, was inspired by an actual visit to the lake. In her book *Poe and the Visual Arts*, Barbara Cantalupo believes Poe could just as easily have seen Chapman's painting of the site, and it is also possible that he merely read Moore's poem.

This means there is at least a chance Poe witnessed the lady of the lake making her nightly rounds. Of course, the "ghost" he and his contemporaries clamored to see was most likely foxfire, a glow created by swamp gases.

part ii

BETWEEN LIFE
AND DEATH

---

*The boundaries which divide Life from Death, are at best shadowy and vague.
Who shall say where the one ends, and where the other begins?*

—*Edgar Allan Poe, "The Premature Burial"*

Chapter 4

LOVE ENTOMBED

P oe nearly died. He lost the power of speech and could barely breathe. The fourteen-year-old almost collapsed at her feet, so overwhelmed was he by his first glimpse of Jane Stanard, the woman he would later term "the first, purely ideal, love of my soul."

At least, that is how he remembered the event a couple decades later. Poe's mother-in-law recalled in an April 14, 1859 letter to Sarah Helen Whitman:

> *This lady, on entering the room, took his hand and spoke some gentle and gracious words of welcome, which so penetrated the sensitive heart of the orphan boy as to deprive him of the power of speech, and, for a time, almost of consciousness itself. He returned home in a dream, with but one thought, one hope in life—to hear again the sweet and gracious words that had made the desolate world so beautiful to him, and filled his lonely heart with the oppression of a new joy. This lady afterwards became the confidant of all his boyish sorrows, and her's was the one redeeming influence that saved and guided him in the earlier days of his turbulent and passionate youth.*

With long dark hair worn in a Scottish snood, porcelain skin and the features of a classical sculpture, Stanard had an otherworldliness about her. Poe rhapsodized about her, his own Helen of Troy, in his early poem "To Helen," in which he found her beauty "like those Nicéan barks of yore

Jane Stanard's grave in Shockoe Hill Cemetery.

which gently o'er a perfumed sea the weary wayward wanderer bore to his own native shore." Her beauty was distant, drawing him across the sea and into her world. In this sense, hers was like the beauty of the mother he had never known, whose likeness he kept in a locket he wore close to his heart. Stanard resembled Poe's mother, who was herself renowned, even revered, for her loveliness.

Of course, there was a problem. Stanard was the happily married mother of one of his classmates, so this could never be anything more than a schoolboy crush. The young poet started carrying his poems to Stanard in hopes of receiving some motherly advice and encouragement, anything to take his mind off the tensions back home. Allan and Poe were arguing more than ever those days, and a fight usually ended with Allan threatening to send the boy adrift. Jane Stanard's mansion overlooking Capitol Square became Poe's refuge. He could confide in her and count on her to comfort him.

Then she died. After a brief lapse into insanity, she succumbed to a mysterious illness at the age of thirty-one. Poe was fifteen, and his world was shattered. One of his friends recalled this period as the only time he knew of Poe being depressed. Even Allan noticed the change, writing to Poe's brother that Edgar "seems quite miserable, sulky & ill-tempered."

Stanard passed at the end of April 1824. Her young admirer spent many a spring night at her grave high above the city in the new Shockoe Hill Cemetery. The burying ground had opened only two years earlier, so the field was only sparsely populated with white marble monuments.

Even in an age when mourning customs were growing more elaborate, when widows hid their faces behind black veils and kept their tears in glass vials called tear catchers for the first year after their husbands died, Poe's mourning for a friend's mother might have seemed excessive.

He was probably not worried about protecting her remains from grave robbers since the Medical College of Virginia had not yet opened or employed a "resurrectionist" to procure fresh cadavers for gross anatomy classes. Some of the leftover bones from these stolen corpses were recently found in a disused well during construction on the campus.

Rather, there was something more akin to obsession about his visits to her grave. As his fiancée, Sarah Helen Whitman, recalled in her biography of the poet:

> *For months after her decease it was his habit to visit nightly the cemetery where the object of his boyish idolatry lay entombed. The thought of*

her—sleeping there in her loneliness—filled his heart with a profound, incommunicable sorrow. When the nights were very dreary and cold, when the autumnal rains fell, and the winds wailed mournfully over the graves, he lingered longest and came away most regretfully.

Whitman's description, probably based on Poe's own words and embellished by her own Spiritualist beliefs, suggests that he felt Jane's presence there—as if she were only sleeping. As he wrote in his early poem "Spirits of the Dead":

THY soul shall find itself alone
'Mid dark thoughts of the gray tomb-stone—
Not one, of all the crowd, to pry
Into thine hour of secrecy…
Be silent in that solitude,
Which is not loneliness—for then
The spirits of the dead who stood
In life before thee are again
In death around thee—and their will
Shall overshadow thee: be still.

Reuniting with dead lovers would become a recurring theme in Poe's tales like "Morella," "Ligeia" and "Eleonora." In stories like "Berenice" and "The Fall of the House of Usher," prematurely entombed women refuse to stay buried. Maybe he was secretly hoping to see Stanard again. As his biographer James Harrison put it, Poe was filled "with the passionate feeling of undying companionship, even with the dead, which afterwards ran like a line of fire through his romances of death, trance, and sentience after death."

Poe soon fell in love again, this time with a girl his own age, Elmira Royster. Once again, their relationship was doomed. Her father disapproved of the match, forcing them to rendezvous in a secluded walled garden, where they became secretly engaged. When Poe left to attend the University of Virginia, her father intercepted the poet's letters to her and convinced her to marry someone else.

After dropping out of college, running away from home, enlisting in the army, getting kicked out of West Point and publishing three volumes of poetry along the way, Poe returned to Richmond at the age of twenty-six to take a position at the *Southern Literary Messenger*. The combined income from his editorial position and his tales enabled him to rent a comfortable room in a boardinghouse on Capitol Square, within sight of Jane Stanard's former home. He married his cousin Virginia Clemm in the boardinghouse's parlor. At the time, she was about the same age Poe had been when he first met Mrs. Stanard, and he was a few years younger than Stanard would have been.

On Sunday afternoons, he and Virginia used to pass the Stanard mansion on the way to Shockoe Hill Cemetery, where he never failed to point out to his bride Helen's grave.

Two centuries after Poe's midnight vigils, one can still visit Shockoe Hill Cemetery, where an old metal sign shows the way to Jane Stanard's monument. On the spot where Poe likely knelt is a small bronze plaque placed there in 1923 by the California psychiatrist, Poe collector and Spiritualist John Wooster Robertson. (There will be more about him in a later chapter.) Robertson was fascinated by the workings of Poe's mind and thought that because Poe's biological mother had left him too early, he was trying to replace her with Jane Stanard. Believing that Poe's poem "The Valley Nis," an early version of "The Valley of Unrest," was inspired by Poe's visits to Stanard's grave, Robertson included some lines from this poem on the plaque. They read:

> *Helen, like thy human eye*
> *There th' uneasy violets lie—*
> *There the reedy grass doth wave*
> *Over the old forgotten grave—*
> *One by one from the tree top*
> *There the eternal dews do drop—*

Since these verses mention violets on a grave, he sent one hundred California violets to Richmond to be planted on Stanard's plot. Unfortunately, there were simply too many for the space. As many as could fit were planted over her remains.

As we have seen, Poe grew up immersed in supernatural legends and beliefs. European and African spiritual beliefs mingled in the Richmond of his youth. As an adult, he saw his world change with the introduction of trains connecting major cities, telegraphs enabling instant communication over vast distances, photography producing instant and accurate likenesses and galvanic piles harnessing the power of electricity. Amid these technological wonders, the old superstitions began to fade away. But the quest to communicate with the dead continued, this time aided by the powers of animal magnetism.

Chapter 5

POE SPEAKS WITH THE DEAD

Never before had a human subject been held in a trance for so long, but the truly remarkable thing, which would capture the world's imagination, was that the mesmerized man had been dead for seven months. In the ultimate test of the hotly debated claims of animal magnetism, Ernest Valdemar allowed himself to be mesmerized on his deathbed by a team of scientists. Half a year later, his body remained suspended in the process of decomposition. His skin was cold and pale, and his heart had long since stopped. But his rotten black tongue continued to vibrate in response to his doctors' questions.

Once Valdemar's corpse was clearly stiff and dry, the mesmerists attempted to wake him from his trance. The frozen jaws and decayed tongue emitted a horrible sound, a voice that seemed to originate from somewhere within the dry throat. "Dead! Dead!" he groaned, begging them to put him out of his misery. As soon as they released Valdemar from their control, his body crumbled into a "nearly liquid mass of loathsome—of detestable putrescence."

The December 1845 issue of the *American Review: A Whig Journal* carried the whole story, and it was almost immediately reprinted in the December 20, 1845 issue of the *Broadway Journal*. The news soon crossed the Atlantic and had people around the world debating its validity and speculating that its author, Edgar Allan Poe, just might have mesmeric powers.

"The Facts in the Case of M. Valdemar" was not the first of Poe's articles to address the theme of mesmerism. A year earlier, he had preceded it with "A Tale of the Ragged Mountains" and "Mesmeric Revelation." The latter records a mesmerist's interview with his entranced subject, who, like Valdemar, has crossed over during his trance.

Mesmerism was a popular pseudoscience of the day. In the closing decades of the previous century, Franz Anton Mesmer developed his theory of "animal magnetism," which claimed that all matter was connected by magnetic fields that could be manipulated by the process of mesmerism (similar to hypnosis) in which the mesmerist could share his magnetic force with a patient in order to cure diseases of the mind or body. During the process, the patient's soul supposedly left his body, allowing him, in theory, to communicate with other disembodied spirits. As Poe explained in a July 2, 1844 letter to James Russell Lowell:

> *At death, the worm is the butterfly—still material, but of a matter unrecognized by our organs—recognized, occasionally, perhaps, by the sleep-waker, directly—without organs—through the mesmeric medium. Thus a sleep-waker may see ghosts. Divested of the rudimental covering, the being inhabits space—what we suppose to be the immaterial universe— passing every where, and acting all things, by mere volition—cognizant of all secrets but that of the nature of God's volition—the motion, or activity, of the unparticled matter.*

After reading Chauncey Hare Townshend's book *Facts in Mesmerism*, Poe hailed it as "one of the most truly profound and philosophical works of the day" in the April 5, 1845 issue of the *Broadway Journal*. A few months later, the same magazine published a letter (which Poe, who worked for the magazine, surely read) by New York's Dr. A. Sidney Doane, who had just performed surgery on a mesmerized patient without the aid of anesthesia. By the time Poe published "Mesmeric Revelation," the public would not only have access to volumes on animal magnetism but could also see one of many traveling quack mesmerists entrancing audiences on both sides of the Atlantic. Scores of mesmerists were even operating out of storefronts or making house calls in major cities.

Anna Cora Mowatt, a popular writer and actress whose performances Poe praised, visited a mesmerist at the suggestion of her physician, Dr. Valentine Mott, who, incidentally, also treated Poe a few years later. Although Mowatt initially underwent hypnosis to treat her tuberculosis, she soon experienced an unusual side effect. While entranced, she found that her personality disappeared to be replaced by "the gypsy," a distinct personality whose activities Mowatt claimed not to remember upon waking. This other being could predict the near future and read people's minds.

Epes Sargent, a witness to her mesmeric treatments, wrote on January 18, 1842, to E.P. Whipple:

> *The magnetic experiments are still continuing, and daily new phenomena are developed. It is rare that a subject reaches the high stage to which she has attained. In her case we see daily proved the most ultra and incredible facts reported of magnetism—facts which we dare not tell her in her waking state nor anyone else—so of this let nothing be intimated. This I tell you, however, as one of the least remarkable. I have conversed mentally with her for several minutes—she replying vocally to my unuttered questions, and sometimes even anticipating my thoughts by placing her hand on my head.*

Given the prevalence of such accounts of mesmeric sessions, it is little wonder that many of Poe's readers took his entirely fictional tales of mesmerism seriously. The editor of the New York *New World* reprinted the "marvelous article" "Mesmeric Revelation" in its August 3, 1844 issue, with the introductory statement that

> *Mr. Poe cannot, on so serious a subject, trifle with his readers: yet more extraordinary statements can hardly be conceived. We do believe in the facts of mesmerism, although we have not yet been able to arrive at any theory sufficient to explain them. Here, however, we are almost staggered.*

The Lowell, Massachusetts *Star of Bethlehem* for October 4, 1845, introduced its own reprint of the story by stating:

> *The following extraordinary article was, we believe, originally published in the "Columbian Magazine." Whether it is a statement of facts, or merely a development of the writer's system of mental philosophy we know not. Be that as it may it is worthy of a careful perusal. The reader can draw his own conclusions.—We give it as it is, without farther comments.*

Poe was soon obliged to answer a few of the public's questions about his mesmeric knowledge. In a letter printed in the April 11, 1846 issue of London's *Popular Record of Modern Science*, Poe explained:

The philosophy detailed in the "Last Conversation of a Somnambule" [the title under which "Mesmeric Revelation" appeared in the *Popular Record of Modern Science*] *is my own—original, I mean, with myself, and had long impressed me. I was anxious to introduce it to the world in a manner that should insure for it attention. I thought that by presenting my speculations in a garb of vraisemblance—giving them as revelations—I would secure for them a hearing, and I depended upon what the Popular Record very properly calls the "Magazinish" tone of the article to correct any false impression which might arise in regard to the question of fact or fable.*

In reference to "The Facts in the Case of M. Valdemar," Poe continued:

In the case of Valdemar, I was actuated by similar motives, but in this latter paper, I made a more pronounced effort at verisimilitude for the sake of effect. The only material difference between the two articles is, that in one I believe actual truth to be involved; in the other I have aimed at merely suggestion and speculation. I find the Valdemar case universally copied and received as truth, even in spite of my disclaimer.

Even more popular than the wildly successful "Mesmeric Revelation," "The Facts in the Case of M. Valdemar" was reprinted in no fewer than ten different magazines within a month of its first publication. It appeared in Europe the following month and reached Australian magazines by the end of the year. London's *Popular Record of Modern Science* featured it as a work of nonfiction in January 1846 because, according to the editor, "credence is understood to be given it at New York.…The angry excitement and various rumors which have at length rendered a public statement necessary, are sufficient to show that something extraordinary must have taken place."

At the same time, London's Short and Co. published "Valdemar" as a pamphlet titled *Mesmerism; In Articulo Mortis* with a title page bearing the description "An Astounding & Horrifying Narrative, Shewing the Extraordinary Power of Mesmerism in Arresting the Progress of Death. By Edgar A. Poe, Esq. of New York." The preface attested that the story was "a plain recital of facts" and that "credence is given to it in America, where the occurrence took place."

Some readers could not resist writing Poe to learn the truth. A month after the story appeared in the *American Review*, the mesmerist Robert Collyer wrote Poe a letter, which the latter reprinted in the *Broadway Journal*:

DEAR SIR—Your account of M. Valdemar's Case has been universally copied in this city, and has created a very great sensation. It requires from me no apology, in stating, that I have not the least doubt of the possibility of such a phenomenon; for, I did actually restore to active animation a person who died from excessive drinking of ardent spirits....I will give you the detailed account on your reply to this, which I require for publication, in order to put at rest the growing impression that your account is merely a splendid creation of your own brain, not having any truth in fact. My dear sir, I have battled the storm of public derision too long on the subject of Mesmerism, to be now found in the rear ranks—though I have not publicly lectured for more than two years, I have steadily made it a subject of deep investigation.

Voicing a decidedly more skeptical opinion on the tale's veracity, the *New-York Tribune* opined:

The article in the American Review *of this month, entitled, "The Facts of M. Valdemar's Case, by EDGAR A. POE," is of course a romance—who could have supposed it otherwise? Those who have read Mr. Poe's visit to the Maelstrom, South Pole, &c., have not been puzzled by it, yet we learn that several good matter-of-fact citizens have been, sorely. It is a pretty good specimen of Poe's style of giving an air of reality to fictions, and we utterly condemn the choice of a subject, but whoever thought it a veracious recital must have the bump of Faith large, very large indeed.*

Even though he had never even claimed "The Fact in the Case of M. Valdemar" was true, Poe could not let the attack go unanswered, writing in the *Broadway Journal*:

For our parts we find it difficult to understand how any dispassionate transcendentalist can doubt the facts as we state them; they are by no means so incredible as the marvels which are hourly narrated, and believed, on the topic of Mesmerism. Why cannot a man's death be postponed indefinitely by Mesmerism? Why cannot a man talk after he is dead? Why?—why?—that is the question; and as soon as the Tribune *has answered it to our satisfaction we will talk to it farther.*

When a Scottish mesmerist wrote Poe, beseeching him, "for the sake of Science and Truth," to reveal whether the story was true, Poe finally admitted, "'Hoax' is precisely the word suited to M. Valdemar's case.... Some few believe it—but I do not—and don't you."

Poe's mesmeric stories had made him the talk of both New York and London, and he was invited to the exclusive literary soirees Anne Charlotte Lynch hosted each week in her Greenwich Village home. Even among the leading writers, artists and politicians mingling at her parties, Poe was the one everyone came to see. His star continued to rise when he read his new poem "The Raven" for her guests. One of the attendees wrote to Poe's future fiancée, Sarah Helen Whitman, "People seem to think there is something uncanny about him, and the strangest stories are told, and, what is more, believed, about his mesmeric experiences, at the mention of which he always smiles."

Chapter 6

POE AND THE BIRTH
OF SPIRITUALISM

T he audience leaned closer to the stage. Without breaking the silence, the legendary Seer of Poughkeepsie, Andrew Jackson Davis, slipped into a trance. Although not yet twenty, this scrawny, unlearned son of a small-town cobbler had commanded respect over the previous year for his mesmeric healing powers. While in a trance state, he was known to dispense remarkably accurate medical advice to his spectators, so this evening, that sophisticated New York City crowd was listening intently for anything the scrawny young clairvoyant with the piercing eyes under a wild tangle of dark hair might tell it. His spirit now temporarily free of his mortal coil, Davis was able to see disembodied spirits who conveyed to him visions of their world—a place he called the Summerland. His faithful transcriber jotted down every word for publication and posterity. Davis was, after all, a prophet ushering in the new age—the epoch of Spiritualism. Watching this spectacle from the back of the room was Edgar Allan Poe.

Within a few decades, millions of devotees would be gathering in darkened parlors to commune with the dead. Their efforts were rewarded with mysterious knockings, rocking tables, messages written by phantom hands and ghostly voices emanating from the ether. Poe's career coincided with the birth of the Spiritualist movement. As a writer keenly attuned to the spirit of his times, he was drawn to incorporate the new religion into his tales and essays. Along the way, he almost accidentally became a

Andrew Jackson Davis.

popularizer of the movement's beliefs, particularly the use of mesmerism to communicate with the spirits of the dead. Some adherents even ascribed to him supernatural powers. And appropriately, his place in the movement became more prominent during his afterlife.

ANY DISCUSSION OF POE'S relationship with Spiritualism must begin with a brief history of the movement. Spiritualism had its roots in the teachings of eighteenth-century Swiss scientist and philosopher Emanuel Swedenborg, who espoused the belief that God occupied all matter, living and inanimate. Of greater interest to the Spiritualists, he claimed to have psychic powers with which he could communicate with disembodied spirits from this and other planets.

Swedenborg's teachings found a receptive audience in the United States during the first half of the nineteenth century when the religious fervor spurred by the Second Great Awakening stirred the public to found a great number of new religious sects, including the Mormons, the Millerites and the Unitarians. Some of these groups professed that the world would end in 1843, while others were willing to break from both Protestantism and Catholicism by writing entirely new religious texts. Describing his visit to antebellum America in *Democracy in America*, Frenchman Alexis de Tocqueville noted, "The sects that exist in the United States are innumerable." The Americans seemed to be starting new religions every week.

Many of those who would eventually join the Spiritualist movement began as Swedenborgians. Poe knew of the philosopher, at least by reputation, as early as 1838, when he included Swedenborg's book *Heaven and Hell* among the mystical tomes in Roderick Usher's library in his tale "The Fall of the House of Usher." Poe scholar Thomas Ollive Mabbott believed the common theme among the volumes compiled in that imaginary library "dealt with ideas about spirit pervading matter, bipart soul, and the relations of microcosm to macrocosm," all themes that would recur in Poe's work, culminating in his magnum opus *Eureka* in 1848.

As a religious movement, Spiritualism traces its birth to March 1848, when Andrew Jackson Davis announced from the stage at one of his public trances in New York City that something had just happened that would transform the world. As if on cue, two young Hydesville, New York sisters, fifteen-year-old Margaret and eleven-year-old Kate Fox, claimed to be engaging in regular communication with the dead. According to the girls, they were able to ask questions of the ghost of a murdered peddler who answered them with knocking sounds. By 1888, when Margaret admitted to having faked those noises, Spiritualism had grown into an international religion. Her confession did nothing to quell the movement's popularity, which exploded during the American Civil War and resurged after the First World War, when countless parents sought connection with loved ones lost in the smoke of battle.

While the Fox sisters were the public face of the new religion, Davis was Spiritualism's first important theologian. He is credited with determining the terminology and underlying principles of the movement, and his writings systematizing and explaining the movement's beliefs became its scripture. He consequently came to be known as the "Saint Paul" or the "John the Baptist" of Spiritualism. In his lifetime, he was also revered as a healer, a mesmerist and the "Poughkeepsie Seer," after his hometown.

Davis's public dialogues with the dead set the standard for generations of supposed mediums, those "sensitives" who deemed themselves the "medium" of communication through which spirits in the afterlife conversed with the living in the physical world. In small gatherings known as séances, believers gathered around such a medium to hear him or her speak in an altered voice supposed to be that of a ghost talking through them. To dazzle and dumbfound the witnesses, the medium might also produce unexplained noises. By the turn of the century, séances could feature such theatrical elements as floating tables, musical instruments playing themselves and glowing figures emerging from cabinets.

In 1844, FOUR YEARS before the Fox sisters' emergence, Davis claimed to have had his initial séance when he entered a trance state in which he communicated with the long-dead Swedenborg and the ancient Greek physician Galen (who died in 210). In November of the following year, Davis held the first of 157 public trance demonstrations in New York.

Poe was residing in New York at the time of Davis's lectures and mentioned Davis in his published writings on two occasions. In the first, the introduction to his satirical short story "Mellonta Tauta," Poe referenced "Martin Van Buren Mavis (sometimes called the 'Toughkeepsie Seer')." In this context, Poe portrayed Davis as, in the words he used to describe the Transcendentalists, "a class of gentlemen with whom we have no patience whatever—the mystics for mysticism's sake."

The second reference appeared in Poe's May 1849 article "Fifty Suggestions." The eleventh "Suggestion" reads, "There surely cannot be more things in Heaven and Earth than are dreamt of (oh, Andrew Jackson Davis!) in your philosophy." Neither of these brief passages gives the impression that Poe took Davis's theories very seriously, even if they intrigued him.

While Davis's staged trances have been credited by Thomas Ollive Mabbott and other Poe scholars with inspiring "The Facts in the Case of M. Valdemar," the composition of "Mesmeric Revelation" preceded them. Even though Poe published the tale before Davis gave his first public demonstration, the theories the mesmerized character in "Mesmeric Revelation" was able to discover while in a trance state are similar to those Davis espoused three years later in his 1847 book *The Principles of Nature, Her Divine Revelations and a Voice to Mankind*. Among these are the presence of the Divine within all matter and the definition of God as unparticled matter. Elsewhere in *The Principles of Nature*, Davis stated, "The ever-controlling influence and active energies of the Divine Positive Mind brought all effects into being, as parts of one vast whole." Mabbott suggested that this, in turn, influenced Poe's book *Eureka*, which is based on the premise that the universe emerged from and will return to a unity, which is one divine mind.

Shortly after its publication, Poe found it necessary to discuss "Mesmeric Revelation" with both Davis and Davis's defender, the Swedenborgian and future Spiritualist George Bush. While Poe insisted that the work was completely fictional, he told both Davis and Bush that it reflected his actual beliefs. On January 4, 1845, Poe sent Bush a copy of the short story, writing:

> *You will, of course, understand that the article is purely a fiction;—but I have embodied in it some thoughts which are original with myself & I am exceedingly anxious to learn if they have claim to absolute originality, and also how far they will strike you as well based. If you would be so kind as to look over the paper and give me, in brief, your opinion, I will consider it a high favor.*

It should be noted that Poe wrote that he considered his theories original, strengthening the argument that Poe was not inspired by Davis's teachings and allowing for the possibility that Davis was at least aware of Poe's work when writing *The Principles of Nature*. While Bush's reply to this note is unknown, Poe bemusedly mentioned in the August 1845 installment of *Marginalia*:

> *The Swedenborgians inform me that they have discovered all that I said in a magazine article entitled "Mesmeric Revelation," to be absolutely true, although at first they were very strongly inclined to doubt my veracity—a thing which, in this particular instance, I never dreamed of not doing myself. The story is a pure fiction from beginning to end.*

Given Poe's seeming ambivalence on mesmerism, Spiritualism and such matters, it is difficult to discern his actual beliefs. To clear up any confusion, Poe explained in an 1844 letter to James Russell Lowell:

> *I have no belief in spirituality. I think the word a mere word. No one has really a conception of spirit. We cannot imagine what is not. We deceive ourselves by the idea of infinitely rarefied matter. Matter escapes the senses by degrees—a stone—a metal—a liquid—the atmosphere—a gas—the luminiferous ether. Beyond this there are other modifications more rare. But to all we attach the notion of a constitution of particles—atomic composition. For this reason only, we think spirit different; for spirit, we say is unparticled, and therefore is not matter. But it is clear that if we proceed sufficiently far in our ideas of rarefaction, we shall arrive at a point where the particles coalesce; for, although the particles be infinite, the infinity of littleness in the spaces between them, is an absurdity.—The unparticled matter, permeating & impelling, all things, is God. Its activity is the thought of God—which creates. Man, and other thinking beings, are individualizations of the unparticled matter. Man exists as a "person," by being clothed with matter (the particled matter) which individualizes him. Thus habited, his life is rudimental. What we call "death" is the painful metamorphosis. The stars are the habitations of rudimental beings. But for the necessity of the rudimental life, there would have been no worlds.*

Three years after his letter to Lowell, Poe finally published his theories about the universe, God, the spirit and everything else in the aforementioned *Eureka*. While the book found admirers among such prominent French literati as Charles Baudelaire and Paul Valery, it sold poorly in both the United States and (in Baudelaire's translation) in France. Long after *Eureka's* commercial failure, it has since been vindicated by critics as a pioneering work of cosmology that solved Olbers' Paradox (why the night sky is dark if it is filled with stars) and proposed early versions of the Big Bang Theory and Chaos Theory.

In 1847, Davis launched the *Univercoelum*, a magazine intended to disseminate his teachings in print. In preparation for its debut, Davis tried to attract famous writers to contribute articles in support of his cause. Although letters housed in the Association for Research and Enlightenment in Virginia Beach reveal that his assistant contacted poet John Greenleaf Whittier, George Bush and others, Davis did not consider Poe for a position. This may sound surprising, both in light of how Poe's popularity might have increased the journal's circulation and given the praise Davis would later bestow upon Poe in the decades following the author's death. Maybe Davis sensed that Poe had never fully embraced Spiritualism.

Although he was never a Swedenborgian or a Spiritualist, Poe was at least acquainted with Davis, as well as with some of the early adherents of the Spiritualist movement, including Bush, Margaret Fuller, Anna Cora Mowatt, Elizabeth Oakes Smith, George W. Eveleth and Sarah Helen Whitman. He was about as close as he could be to the heart of the movement without actually joining it.

WHILE HE DID NOT write about Poe (or respond to Poe's ridicule of him) during the author's lifetime, Andrew Jackson Davis adopted the deceased poet into the Spiritualist movement. In 1857, Davis released his autobiography, *The Magic Staff*, which includes a description of a meeting with Poe, who discusses "Mesmeric Revelation":

> *Shortly after this pleasant visitation, another gentleman arrived on a similar errand. His remarkable face bore traces of feminine mental characteristics; but upon his spacious brow there sparkled the gems of rare endowments. In his critical eye, however, I observed an ominous shadow! Thinking to myself, I said: "This person's talent immolates his genius." At length he informed us that his name was "Edgar A. Poe." During an interior conversation, I recollect of assuring him that, though he had imagined the whole of his published article upon the answers of a clairvoyant, the main ideas conveyed by it concerning "ultimates" were strictly and philosophically true. At the close of this interview he departed, and never came again.*

As mentioned earlier, Davis did not consider Poe as a contributor to his magazine, but after the author's death, Poe and his works could be utilized to promote the Spiritualist cause. "Mesmeric Revelation," in particular, was considered a revelation of Spiritualist theology. As Davis wrote in his 1868 book *Answers to Ever-Recurring Questions from the People: A Sequel to the Penetralia*: "We have affirmed on two or three occasions, previous to the interview with the gifted poet, that the philosophy of ultimates, unparticled matter, etc., (as set forth by the clairvoyant in Poe's article) was a true philosophy."

In his 1887 book *Events in the Life of a Seer, Being Memoranda of Authentic Facts in Magnetism, Clairvoyance, Spiritualism*, Davis again describes his supposed Poe meeting, this time bestowing upon Poe a "commanding power":

Edgar A. Poe's personal presence conveys me, in feeling, to a beauteous field, or to a kind of blooming valley, surrounded by a high wall of craggy mountains. So high appear these mountains that the sun can scarcely shine over their summits during any portion of the twenty-four hours. There is, too, something unnatural in his voice, and something dispossessing in his manners. He is, in spirit, a foreigner. My sympathies are strangely excited. There are conflicting breathings of commanding power in his mind. But as he walked in through the hall, and again when he left, at the conclusion of his call, I saw a perfect shadow of himself in the air in front of him, as though the sun was constantly shining behind and casting shadows before him, causing the singular appearance of one walking into a dark fog produced by himself.

While Poe had intended his works to entertain readers, rather than to promote any belief system, the Spiritualists embraced both "Mesmeric Revelation" and "The Facts in the Case of M. Valdemar" for the very purpose of popularizing their religion. Given their widespread distribution through reprintings in magazines and newspapers on both sides of the Atlantic, the stories undoubtedly saw a larger readership than any of Andrew Jackson Davis's books or the *Univercoelum*. As works of fiction, these tales were able to package their ideas in a form more palatable to non-initiates than Davis's verbose, jargon-filled tomes. If Poe had chosen to join Davis's movement, he could have been one of its most popular proponents, but he probably did as much as Davis ever did to disseminate their teachings without even trying. He might even have inspired Davis to write a few of those teachings.

Eight decades later, Poe's relationship with Davis earned a brief mention in the twentieth-century Spiritualist and Sherlock Holmes creator Arthur Conan Doyle's book *The History of Spiritualism*. This was followed by John Wooster Robertson's writings attempting to solidify the poet's place in the movement. There will be more about the latter in a later chapter.

Chapter 7

POE'S SOULMATE

W ith all the rumors about Poe's supernatural powers spreading among the literati, it was only a matter of time until he came to the attention of the Providence, Rhode Island poet and Spiritualist Sarah Helen Whitman.

The three years since the publication of "The Facts in the Case of M. Valdemar" had grown progressively desperate for Poe. The celebrity he had enjoyed since the publication of "Valdemar" and "The Raven" in 1845 had allowed him to acquire part ownership of the *Broadway Journal*. Within months, the magazine failed, and his flirtatious relationship with the New York poet Frances Sargent Osgood led to accusations of an extramarital affair. The scandal came to a head when society hostess Anne Charlotte Lynch and a delegation of his friends showed up at Poe's house to demand the return of all the love letters Osgood had sent him. In response, he informed them that their friend Elizabeth Ellet had better worry about the letters *she* was sending him.

Almost overnight, Poe's former friends turned on him. Ellet's brother tried to threaten Poe into retracting what he had said about her, so Poe challenged him to a duel. Since he did not have a pistol for the duel, Poe called on his acquaintance Thomas Dunn English, who ended up getting into a fistfight with him.

On Valentine's Day 1846, with seemingly all of New York's literati against him, Poe's wife presented him with a poem that beseeched him to leave the

Edgar Allan Poe's cottage in Fordham from an 1884 photograph by Arthur Stongton.

city where "the tattling of many tongues" had made life unbearable. She wished to move to a cottage in the country, where the fresh air would "heal [her] weakened lungs."

Within months, they had moved into a tiny white cottage near the village of Fordham, in what is now the Bronx. There, hidden among the rolling hills and cherry trees, Virginia's health continued to decline. At the urging of Poe's admirers, a nurse named Marie Louise Shew volunteered her services to care for Virginia, but it was no use. Poe's wife died at the beginning of 1847.

Her death broke him. Even with Shew continuing to nurse him through his darkest days, he was falling apart. At length, he threw himself into a new venture, the magnum opus he believed would revolutionize science, religion and everything else. In the book's opening sentences, he declared, "I design to speak of the Physical, Metaphysical and Mathematical—of the Material and Spiritual Universe:—of its Essence, its Origin, its Creation, its Present Condition and its Destiny."

Eureka is Poe's attempt to make sense of a world that would cause his beloved Virginia to suffer while the wicked prosper. He proposed that the universe was a work of art—a poem whose plot was so perfectly crafted that cause is indistinguishable from effect. In his view, everything was unified, having come out of the unity to which it would return. Simply put, all matter, energy, time and space were once combined into one particle so dense that it did not exist. His reasoning was that if all particles of matter were combined into one, there would be no energy attracting or repulsing the particles, so there would be no energy. With no energy, there would be no matter. With no matter, there would be no space. With no space, there would be no time. So, before the big bang there was nothing. (Keep in mind that the Belgian priest and cosmologist Georges Lemaître would not propose the Big Bang Theory for another eighty years.) After Poe's big bang expanded the universe to its limit, the whole universe would contract back into itself, eventually collapsing back into nothingness. Then another universe would spring out of nothingness and eventually collapse back into nothingness. Poe imagined an infinite number of these multiple universes, springing in and out of existence. Even more than that, he believed that, as children, we retain vague memories of our previous lives in those other universes.

This idea flew in the face of both accepted Christian beliefs and the then-popular nebular hypothesis of the universe's creation. But it turned truly blasphemous when Poe wrote that, before the big bang and after the big crunch, all matter, energy, spirits and everything else was one—was God. Poe's proof was that it is impossible to believe anyone could be superior to oneself.

After reading *Eureka*, Shew's spiritual advisor, a young theology student named John Henry Hopkins, warned her that continued association with Poe could lead to her eternal damnation. She wrote Poe to tell him she could never see him again.

Hopkins visited Poe in a last effort to dissuade him from his pantheism, but Poe rebuffed him by declaring, "My whole nature utterly revolts at the idea that there is any Being in the Universe superior to myself!" Hopkins gave up on trying to save the poet's soul after that.

Without Shew's friendship, Poe sank into depression once again. But this time, he rebounded. His prospects were looking better than they had in years. He had developed a reputation as a lecturer and received invitations to speak in various cities along the coast. He had also issued a prospectus for a new literary magazine to be called the *Stylus* and was busy courting backers and selling subscriptions for it.

In the process of lecturing and soliciting investors for the *Stylus*, Poe visited Lowell, Massachusetts, where he fell in love with Nancy "Annie" Richmond, the subject of his poem "For Annie." She seemed perfect for him. She was kind, compassionate and nothing like the gossip-mongering literary ladies he had known in New York. She might have reminded him of Virginia, who had been about Annie's age when she died. Annie would have been perfect—if not for her husband.

Poe's travels brought him to Richmond, where a friend informed him that his old flame Elmira Royster was available. At least she was not married, her husband having died five years earlier, but she was less than thrilled to see Poe turning up unannounced on her doorstep one Sunday morning.

He looked up at her from the porch to say, "Elmira, is that you?" only to be informed that she was on her way to church and had no time to speak with him. They had both matured a great deal since those passionate days of their first engagement nearly a lifetime earlier. He looked much older and wearier than his thirty-nine years. She was a prim and proper widow, conscious of how association with the scandal-plagued writer might damage her reputation. Her lips had thinned a bit. Her face was marked by a few more fine lines than he remembered. Her hair was parted and pulled tightly back. But her eyes were as warm and expressive as ever. She might still have been the Elmira he had loved in his youth, but she no longer had time for him.

His Richmond stop was not going as planned. Although he arranged to have the *Southern Literary Messenger* publish some of his unsold essays, he also challenged a rival editor to a duel, and one account has him reciting passages from *Eureka* from atop a marble-top table in one of the seediest bars in Rockett's Landing to whatever drunken sailors happened to be in earshot. No doubt, this audience cared about as much for his theories as Hopkins had.

Just when all seemed lost, Poe received a six-line poem from Sarah Helen Whitman. Although they had never met, the two had been engaged in a literary flirtation since earlier that year. It began in February, when Lynch invited Whitman to send a poem to be read at her annual Valentine's Day soiree, at which the guests would read their verses aloud. As soon as Lynch saw the title of Whitman's contribution, she knew she could not read it, for fear that some of her other guests would no longer associate with her.

Whitman's "To Edgar A. Poe" was addressed to a man no longer welcome in polite New York society. When Lynch had the evening's poetry published in the *Home Journal*, she excluded Whitman's contribution, later explaining to the author that Poe had done "a great many abominable things."

Lynch did, however, forward the manuscript to Frances Osgood, who sent it to Poe. Somehow recognizing her handwriting from a manuscript he had happened to see three years earlier, Poe sent Whitman

Portrait of Sarah Helen Whitman in the guise of the bust of Pallas from Poe's "The Raven."

a response. He tore a copy of his seventeen-year-old poem "To Helen" out of a book and mailed it to her. Whitman's middle name, after all, was Helen.

Within a few months, he sent her a new poem in which he claimed that he had seen her, years earlier, on a trip to Providence. In passing her house one moonlit summer evening, he glimpsed her, glowing in a long white dress as she reclined among the "upturn'd faces of a thousand roses" in her backyard flower garden. Her eyes shone like the stars so that, even years later, he could still see them.

He mailed the poem unsigned and untitled with no return address, but she instantly recognized his handwriting from his earlier letter.

Her reply was the short poem that reached him in Richmond. He could have written her to arrange a meeting like a normal person, but instead, he decided to send a letter under the name Edward S.T. Grey, as if she would not remember his handwriting from the last two letters. It was really just a ploy to find out if she would be home in time for him to meet her in Providence. Within a couple weeks, he showed up at her door with a letter of introduction from a common acquaintance.

She seemed perfect for him, fascinated as she was by mysticism, transcendentalism and the occult. Even out of the moonlight, there was something otherworldly about her. Abundant brown curls framed those luminous blue eyes that had haunted him for the past few years. Her expression, as preserved in photographs, seemed focused on something beyond this world, just out of view of mere mortals. Her mind was so attuned to the latest explorations of the other side that she became an eager and early devotee of Spiritualism.

She could not have been more different from Virginia and Annie. Whitman was six years his senior and a widow. An accomplished poet, she was well known in the Boston and New York literary scenes. A hypochondriac, she kept ether on hand in case her heart got overly excited.

By this time, Whitman had been researching Poe for months, digging up any information she could find on the mysterious, romantic author. She had heard accounts out of New York that he was capable of mesmerism. Frances Osgood warned her, "May Providence protect you if [Poe] has [reached you]!—for his croak [is] the most eloquent imaginable. He is in truth 'A glorious devil, with large heart & brain.'"

Whitman either ignored the warnings or was intrigued by them. She believed there must be a mystical connection between them and had even developed a theory that her maiden name of Power had derived from *Poer*, the root of the Poe surname. He explained, that, if her maiden name were Sarah Helen Poer (rather than Power), this would be an anagram for "Ah, Seraph Lenore." This was not the only encoded sign he found to reveal that they were soulmates.

Showing her his early tale "Morella," about a woman who survives the death of her body by taking over that of her newborn daughter, Poe told Whitman that she was the reincarnation of his beloved Jane Stanard. More than that, she was the "Lost Lenore" of his poem "The Raven." As if in explanation, he wrote, "Robert Stannard Helen Stannard Helen Whitman— Helen Ellen Elenore Lenore!"

Then she described an amazing new unsigned poem she had read in the *American Review*. She had shown "Ulalume" to all of her friends, inquiring about the identity of its author. This strange composition about a man guided through the forest at night by a spirit who brings him to the grave of his lost love, who had died on that very night of the previous year, contained almost indecipherable symbolism buried within its haunting imagery and beautiful rhythm. Although hindsight tells us that only one American poet *could* have written this gloomy verse, she was surprised to learn that she was standing in the presence of its author.

On top of that, she found special significance in the coincidence that they were both born on January 19. All the signs and stars seemed to be drawing them together. Almost all of them, at least. Her overbearing widowed mother and mentally ill sister, who had once been hospitalized for "acute mania," stood in the way.

The first evening Poe and Whitman spent together, she paced her parlor, unwilling to sit next to him for long. On their second meeting, the following day, he took her on a romantic walk in the most appropriate spot for two such dark souls—the local cemetery. There, he told her of Jane Stanard's death while she reclined next to a grave to read one of her poems about a deceased loved one. It was among the gray tombstones of the Swan Point Cemetery that he first professed his love for her, declaring, "Helen, I love you now—now—for the first and only time," tears streaming down his cheeks. But she was not prepared to reciprocate his feelings as long as her mother and sister resisted the match.

Despite their objections, she could not stop seeing him. Believing that Poe possessed supernatural powers, she wrote in her 1860 biography *Edgar Poe and His Critics* that his "mental and temperamental idiosyncrasies fitted him to come readily into rapport with psychal and spiritual influences." Whitman declared that there was "a degree of truth" in his supernatural tales "which he was unwilling to avow." In other words, Poe did not need to believe in the truth of his stories in order for them to be true.

Poe later displayed his clairvoyant powers during a gathering at Whitman's home. John Wooster Robertson's *Edgar Allan Poe: A Psychopathic Study* records an account of that gathering recalled by Whitman's friend Mrs. J.K. Barney. The guests fell suddenly silent while

> *all were drawn toward Poe, whose eyes were gleaming....His eyes were fixed on Mrs. Whitman....Poe stopped talking, keeping his eyes on [her].... Simultaneously both rose from their chairs and walked toward the center of the room. Meeting he held her in his arms, kissed her; they stood for a moment, then he led her to her seat.*

The entire company remained completely silent, under Poe's control, "through all this strange proceeding."

As their relationship progressed, Poe insisted that they be married right away. After one too many of her rejections, he swallowed what should have been a lethal dose of laudanum, a mixture of opium and alcohol. It might have killed him if he had not vomited up the drug.

Less than two weeks later, they were engaged. Her one condition was that he never touch alcohol again.

The engagement lasted one month. Despite his pleas for her to give him just one more chance to prove his devotion, she inhaled some of her ether and collapsed onto her couch, losing consciousness as her mother escorted him out the front door.

Although they would never meet again (at least on this side), she remained his steadfast supporter. After his death, her writings about him were colored by her mystical beliefs and her conviction that Poe possessed supernatural power. In *Edgar Poe and His Critics*, she writes:

> *Edgar Poe's dreams were assuredly often presageful and significant, and while he but dimly apprehended through the higher reason the truths which they foreshadowed, he riveted public attention upon them by the strange fascination of his style, the fine analytical temper of his intellect, and, above all, by the weird splendors of his imagination, compelling men to read and to accredit as possible truths his most marvelous conceptions. He often spoke of the imageries and incidents of his inner life as more vivid and veritable than those of his outer experience.*

She found his mind "rarely gifted, and accessible from peculiarities of psychal and physical organization to the subtle vibrations of an ethereal medium conveying but feeble impressions to the senses of ordinary persons." To her, he was a medium, just as she would soon become. She believed that he shared with her a desire

> *to solve the problem of that phantasmal Shadow-Land, which, through a class of phenomena unprecedented in the world's history, was about to attest itself as an actual plane of conscious and progressive life, the mode and measure of whose relations with our own are already recognised as legitimate objects of scientific research by the most candid and competent thinkers of our time.*

In other words, Poe had been a seeker of life beyond death, of worlds beyond our own, a Spiritualist before Spiritualism.

Chapter 8

POE'S SPIRIT VISITOR

Philadelphia's immaculate street grid glistened under the cerulean sky. Long at the forefront of science, medicine and the arts, the Athens of America had nurtured Poe's creativity during the six years he lived there, and he still had plenty of friends in the area.

But now everybody was gone. Those who could afford to leave had fled, and those with nowhere else to go were huddled indoors. A miasma had settled on the city, seeping through the shuttered windows and bolted doors. The cholera was back. Not quite a generation ago, it had ravaged the globe, sweeping away millions from India to Mexico. Its victims suffered fever, abdominal pain and such incessant diarrhea that they poured out gallons of fluids until their skin turned bluish gray, their fingers and toes shriveled, their faces sunk as if reverting to skeletal form and their organs failed.

The causes were unclear. Doctors speculated it could be divine justice for low living and heavy drinking. Broadsides urged citizens to avoid alcohol and drink more water.

The cures, however, were plenty. The experts prescribed drinks containing ground deer antler, manure, turpentine or mercury, but everyone knew the only real cure was to run as far away as possible.

Poe's train rumbled into Philadelphia in a cloud of smoke and coal dust. He leapt off the car to find his luggage. Glancing across the platform, he caught sight of the two ruffians who had been conspiring against him on the ride from New York. They pretended not to notice him now, but he knew their intentions. His sense of hearing was especially acute. He'd heard it all. They wanted him dead.

There! The porter dropped Poe's luggage on the platform—or at least some of his luggage. He could see the trunk containing his clothes and mirror, but the valise that held his lecture—the one he was going to deliver to raise money for his new magazine venture—was missing. He rummaged among the luggage for it. His whole trip depended on finding this lecture.

After running from one pile of luggage to the next, checking under, over and around, everything in sight, he chased down departing passengers in search of that valise. It was gone. It was over.

He slunk out the door and shuffled down the street, barely able to lift his feet off the ground. The scorching hot cobblestones stung his foot through the hole in his right shoe. Without taking his eyes off the ground, he let his feet lead him, as if by instinct, to a tavern he'd known from the old days. If anyone had asked him—even if he'd asked himself—he would have said the last thing he needed was a drink. A glass of wine was enough to put him under the table, and with his mother-in-law back in Fordham, there was nobody around to miss him or to drag him back home if he succumbed to temptation. It had been nearly eight months since he'd had a drink, the one that had wrecked his chances with Sarah Helen Whitman. By the time he convinced himself that no good could ever come of this, the stein was already in his hand. He spent a few deep breaths studying the bubbles glistening in the gleam that floated through the dust-covered barroom window. Then he took the plunge.

A year earlier, in a January 4, 1848 letter to George W. Eveleth, Poe explained that when reality became unbearable, drink was his only escape, even it was killing him:

> *I am constitutionally sensitive—nervous in a very unusual degree. I became insane, with long intervals of horrible sanity. During these fits of absolute unconsciousness I drank, God only knows how often or how much. As a matter of course, my enemies referred the insanity to the drink rather than the drink to the insanity.*

By the time the night was over, Poe was in Moyamensing Prison, that Gothic fortress whose very shadow would scare the bad right out of any potential criminals. He stumbled across the granite floor to collapse onto what passed for a cot. He wiped the sweat from his forehead. Then his teeth rattled and his body shook. No matter how hard he tried to force himself to

Moyamensing Prison from a nineteenth-century engraving.

hold still or to rub some warmth into his arms, he couldn't stop shivering. Turning onto his side and pulling his knees toward his chest, he clutched his stomach. The pain hit his gut like a ton of bricks. A spasm nearly shook him off the side of the bed. The cholera had found him.

Poe extracted a delicate little bottle from his waistcoat pocket, uncorked it and dropped a couple calomel pills into his palm. Tossing them down his throat, he struggled to swallow. He later wrote that he didn't know what made him sicker—the cholera or the calomel.

A spasm threw him to the floor, where he scrambled on all fours to the chamber pot and vomited. He grasped the edges. His head was being pulled down into the pot, but the stench was just enough to hold him back.

He rolled back onto the cot. Exactly what happened next depends on who is telling the story. The Philadelphia printer and publisher John Sartain, whom Poe encountered a few days later, recalled in the March 1889 issue of *Lippincott's* that Poe was looking at one of the prison's towers through the bars of his window when a radiant young woman alighted atop the coping. She shined so brightly that the bars cast shadows across his cell. From her remote position, she presented him with riddles in a low, soft voice that only his superhuman hearing allowed him to discern. His life depended on giving the correct answers. Regrettably, Sartain had forgotten those questions by the time he related the story forty years later.

Writing of the event in *Laurel Leaves* in 1876, William Fearing Gill, who must have relied on Sartain as his source, recalled that this figure had been a "guardian angel" who "sought to dissuade him from a frightful purpose." This, however, was not the only version of the night's events.

Recalling the same episode about eleven years after the fact for his lecture *The Genius and Character of Edgar Allan Poe*, Richmond magazine editor John Reuben Thompson said that Poe told him that the seraphic figure entered his cell and took him by the hand, leading him up over the tower and into the night sky. They were hovering well above the decimated city by the time Poe realized the woman had transformed into an immense bird with ebony wings blacking out the night sky. This creature croaked, "I am the Cholera!" before throwing off its rider, who felt every bit of the terror of plummeting from that lofty height—only to find himself back in his cell. As he told Thompson a few weeks later, "I could not shake off the conviction that I was the minister of the pestilence that then raged in Philadelphia, and that the death of every one of its victims would be fastened upon my soul."

Poe insisted to Thompson that it was not a dream—that he had been wide awake the entire time. Naturally, both Sartain and Thompson assumed that this had merely been a hallucination, probably brought about by delirium tremens, but the Spiritualist and Poe collector John Wooster Robertson considered it a true case of a spirit visitation.

Thompson delivered his previously mentioned lecture about Poe to audiences familiar with Spiritualism, and some of them, no doubt, would have shared Robertson's opinion of it being a true ghost story rather than an alcohol-induced fever dream.

If Poe spent a night in prison, he was probably released the next morning. Sartain recounted that, recognizing the great poet by name, the mayor of Philadelphia freed Poe, who eventually found his way to Sartain's studio.

Chapter 9

OMENS OF POE'S DEATH

British-born printer John Sartain had mastered the demanding technique of mezzotint engraving to the extent that the images he burned into metal plates using precise acid mixtures could rival the most lifelike photographs of the day.

A barrage of thumps rattled his studio door. The visitor yanked the locked doorknob before pounding the door again. Even as Sartain walked across the room, assuring his unscheduled guest that he was coming, the knocks came quicker, louder, more desperate.

As soon as Sartain undid the latch, the visitor fell into the room, catching himself on Sartain's shoulder as the door slammed against the wall. It took a moment for Sartain to recognize the haggard face. It looked like someone he'd known—if that someone had been through a hurricane. The visitor's pale face glistened. His hair stood on end. His eyes were wild.

"Poe," said Sartain. "Is that you?"

Sartain recalled the day's events four decades later in his previously mentioned *Lippincott's Magazine* article. Poe told him of hearing two passengers conspiring against him on the train. These villains did not realize that Poe had exceptional hearing and had anticipated their evil intentions. But now they were after him. When Sartain asked why anyone would want to harm him, Poe answered, "Well, a woman trouble."

Poe begged Sartain for a razor to shave off his mustache so they would not recognize him. Worried that Poe might slash his own throat with such a blade, Sartain offered to trim Poe's facial hair with scissors. This seemed to work. Poe calmed down and caught some rest in the studio while Sartain got back to work on his printing plates.

Night fell, and the day's stifling heat subsided. Poe stepped outside, but still fearing that the poet might harm himself, the printer insisted on joining him. The two took an omnibus across town to the Fairmount Waterworks, where Poe climbed the stairs to the reservoir high above the Schuylkill River, where the Philadelphia Museum of Art now stands. All the while, Sartain hurried to keep up—and to place himself between his friend and the ledge.

When they reached the summit, the men sat together in total darkness. There was no moon, and the clouds blocked out even the stars' dim twinkle. In the impenetrable blackness, Poe recounted the previous night's vision in the prison cell and described the demonic men who had tortured him. First, they tried to make him drink from a boiling cauldron. Then they forced him to watch as they dismembered his beloved mother-in-law.

In an 1895 letter in the Poe Museum's collection, Sartain stated that throughout the evening, Poe was measured and deliberate in everything he said. To Sartain, Poe did not appear to be suffering from the influence of drugs or alcohol. Just what caused these horrifying visions is anyone's guess.

The next day, Poe returned to his normal self and admitted that everything had been a hallucination. He may have been far from well, but he was recovering. Still, he could not shake the premonition that he would soon be dead. He wrote to Maria Clemm, "We can but die together. It is no use to reason with me now; I must die. I have no desire to live since I have done 'Eureka.' I could accomplish nothing more. For your sake it would be sweet to live, but we must die together."

Somehow, Poe knew he would never see her again. But this did not deter him from his plans.

Thanks to some loans from friends, Poe was able to reach Richmond a week later, still too ill to write home to his mother-in-law. After a gradual improvement, during which his physician warned him that another drop of wine would kill him, Poe was ready to get back to business. As he had done the previous summer, he connected with John R. Thompson at the *Southern Literary Messenger* to arrange the publication of more of his articles. Poe was also rounding up financial backers and selling subscriptions for the *Stylus*, and he gave public lectures and readings in Richmond and Norfolk.

Just as importantly, he was visiting Elmira Shelton at her Church Hill mansion in hopes of renewing their relationship. She was still living there with her ten-year-old son Southall and a few servants. Since her husband's death, she had generated a small fortune from her rental properties. Even though her late husband had sought to discourage gold diggers by stipulating in his will that she would lose two-thirds of her inheritance upon remarrying, she would still retain just enough to provide a comfortable lifestyle for herself, Edgar and Southall. Before the leaves turned, they were engaged. Poe wrote to Maria Clemm that their money problems were almost over.

This is not to imply that Poe did not hold a genuine affection for Elmira. He wrote to Maria Clemm, "I think she loves me more devotedly than any one I ever knew & I cannot help loving her in return."

He did, however, still have his doubts. In his letters to Clemm, the poet bemoaned the fact that he could never be with Annie Richmond. At the end of August, he wrote, "My love for [Annie] will never, never cease, either in this world or the next."

Within weeks of writing those words, he was resolved to marry Shelton and wanted Clemm to stop sending him news of Annie. "Do not tell me anything about Annie," he wrote. "I cannot bear to hear it now—unless you can tell me that Mr. R. is dead."

For her part, Shelton was committed to marriage. She was willing to give up a portion of her inheritance, to move Maria Clemm into her home and to relocate with Poe to the North to escape her disapproving relatives, who were urging her not to throw her life away by marrying a penniless poet.

Poe's sacrifice for Shelton was probably just as difficult. He joined the Sons of Temperance, a group whose members pledged to abstain from alcohol. His enlistment would not only prove his devotion to Shelton in a way he never could for Whitman, but it also might just save his life.

The poet's lectures and readings were warmly received. A financial backer from Illinois was prepared to help Poe finally launch the *Stylus*. Some accounts have it that he sold enough subscriptions to publish the first issue. With his wedding to Elmira set for October 17, he had every reason to be happy, but he could not escape that sense of foreboding.

Two nights before he left Richmond, he gave a final private reading at a farmhouse called Talavera on the western outskirts of the city. Susan Archer Talley, who lived there with her parents, was a poet, an admirer of Poe's works and a friend of the poet's sister, who happened to be her neighbor. On the first floor, just to the right of the entrance, pocket doors opened onto a small parlor where the Talleys and a few guests gathered around the fireplace where Poe stood, stiff as a board, with one hand resting on the mantel and the other holding a thin paper scroll just high enough for him to read the verses of "The Raven." He was so focused that he ignored the moth fluttering about his face as he performed.

Talavera in its present location.

Susan Talley had quizzed him all summer for every detail about that poem. He had told her, for example, that he had originally considered writing about an owl instead. Half a century later, she wrote a biography of Poe and composed several articles about him and his visits with her. These accounts provided the details of his last reading.

Almost totally deaf by this time, she must have listened to his reading through a funnel held up to her ear. Seated near her, Rosalie Poe could barely contain her excitement. The servants piled into the hallway to listen through the door.

Poe was so aware of the music of his poetry that he nearly sang the work, entrancing his audience, drawing them deeper under his spell with each syllable. Then the volume increased, rising to a crescendo with the impassioned line, "Get thee back into the tempest and the Night's Plutonian Shore!" At this, some of the children scurried down the hallway.

At the recital's conclusion, Poe intoned those most melancholy words, "And my soul from out that shadow that lies floating on the floor/ Shall be lifted Nevermore." The whole house fell silent.

As if on cue, Rosalie hopped onto Poe's lap. The room burst into laughter when he joked that he should bring her to all his readings—to play the part of the raven.

When Poe departed that evening, he stepped out the front door and turned to Susan to thank her for her hospitality. He was about to travel to Philadelphia and New York in a couple days but intended to return soon with Maria Clemm to attend his wedding.

Just then, a shooting star illuminated the sky behind him. Attuned as they were to signs and omens, they knew that someone's death was imminent.

The next evening, Elmira Shelton also feared for Poe's life but for less supernatural reasons. She found him to be dizzy and feverish. His pulse was weak, and he was paler than usual. Some who have compared the daguerreotype taken of Poe at about that time with one for which he sat a year earlier in Providence believe he had visibly lost weight and grown more haggard and wearier over that period. Something was killing him.

Although she pleaded with him to stay, he insisted on taking the early morning steamship to Norfolk. From there, he would board another ship to Baltimore to catch a train to Philadelphia, where he had a lucrative editing assignment waiting for him. Then he would head to New York to take Maria Clemm back with him to Richmond for his wedding.

The next morning, Shelton hurried to Rockett's Landing in hopes of stopping him before his ship departed, but it was too late. Within a week, he was found at a Baltimore polling place on election day, semiconscious

Washington College Hospital, where Poe breathed his last.

and dressed in someone else's clothes. An old acquaintance of his from the magazine business sent him to a nearby hospital, but Poe had no memory of how he got there. Over the course of four days, Poe alternated between active delirium and rest. His attending physician claimed that the hallucinating poet engaged in "constant talking—and vacant converse with spectral and imaginary objects on the walls." At one point, Poe screamed the name "Reynolds!" repeatedly until late into the night. Then he calmed and declared, "Lord, help my poor soul," before crossing over to the other side.

Some of his relatives buried him the next day in an unmarked grave in a Baltimore burying ground. Maria Clemm, Rosalie Poe, Annie Richmond, Sarah Helen Whitman and Elmira Shelton did not learn of his death until later, when they read about it in the paper.

Clemm might have noticed another omen—Poe's beloved cat Caterina had died on October 7, the day of the poet's death.

Chapter 10

POE SPEAKS FROM
BEYOND THE GRAVE

The autumn of Poe's death had turned to winter, and the last red and golden leaves had fallen from the trees in Providence. The rose bushes behind Sarah Helen Whitman's house had long since shed their petals, but she could not see that. The curtains were all drawn, shutting out the physical world. The chamber was illuminated by the faint red light from a gas lamp covered with crimson glass. This gave the room the ideal unearthly, otherworldly glow appropriate for someone like her, who dwelt in the realm of spirits.

Almost a year had passed since she last saw him, but now that he had crossed over from the earthly plane, she could sense his presence more clearly, more tangibly, than ever. She habitually fell into an interior conversation with him, thinking the things she could have said or should have said when she had the chance. It always ended the same way, with the sting of regret, that deep body ache that resonated within her when she paused just long enough to let a grain of the real world seep into her one-sided conversation. Then it hit her, as it always did, that he was gone, that she was conversing with nothing more than memories and shadows.

She wondered if he had forgiven her. Then there was a knock on the back of her chair. It startled her for just long enough for her to realize that she hadn't breathed or even moved since her initial gasp. She did not need to turn to know there was nobody standing behind her. She had not even heard any footsteps in the hallway.

Sarah Helen Whitman during a séance.

Without uttering a word, she asked herself if it could have been him. Another knock sounded, but this time it was in front of her—seemingly in the middle of her table. "Edgar?" she asked. Something, somewhere answered with a knock.

This is how Whitman claimed she reunited with Poe's spirit. Of course, she would need some help facilitating their communication, so she hired a professional medium, a sensitive named "M," to move into her home for six weeks. She then brought in the trance poet Sarah Gould to assist her. Poe's spirit apparently dictated to her the message, "Pray for me, Helen, pray for me."

After Gould's departure, Whitman became a medium herself. Though she admitted to never actually seeing a ghost, she related that she had seen a spirit hand write "three initial letters." On another occasion, while staring at a portrait of Poe, Whitman wrote the lines beginning "After long years I raised the fold concealing/ That face, magnetic as the morning's beam:/ While slumbering memory thrilled at its revealing."

Whitman's claims became so well known in Spiritualist circles that she received requests from Poe's admirers asking her to send the deceased author questions. George Eveleth, a former correspondent of Poe's, asked Whitman to communicate with the author on his behalf and to relay "whatever revelations she might obtain." Eveleth wrote to one of the author's acquaintances that Poe "hasn't let go even yet, but is managing at his pleasure, through the medium of the Spirit Telegraph with Mrs. Whitman at t'other end of the wire."

COMMUNION WITH POE'S SPIRIT seemed especially popular with mediums in the period immediately following his death. Two years after Poe's passing, the trance medium Lydia M. Kenney wrote "Poe in Heaven," a poem she claimed to have received from his spirit, which she published in the January 15, 1852 issue of *The Spirit Messenger*. In 1857, Dr. J.J. Garth Wilkinson released *Improvisations of the Spirit*, a book of poetry supposedly given to him from the spirit world. Among the verses he received were six pages from Edgar Allan Poe.

In 1863, the medium Lizzie Doten published the collection *Poems of the Inner Life*, which contains poetry she claimed was dictated to her by the spirits of famous writers. Six of the poems were supposedly written by Poe's spirit. With titles like "The Streets of Baltimore" and "The Cradle or Coffin," these verses were merely pastiches of Poe's writing style. She, however, claimed not to have read any of his poems except "The Raven." Rather, she insisted that when "under the influence of Poe, [she] would awaken in the night from a deep slumber, and detached fragments of those poems would be floating through [her] mind."

She found communication with Poe to be "neither pleasant nor easy."

I can only describe it as a species of mental intoxication. I was tortured with a feeling of great restlessness and irritability, and strange, incongruous images crowded my brain. Some were bewildering and dazzling as the sun, others dark and repulsive. Under his influence, particularly, I suffered the greatest exhaustion of vital energy, so much so, that after giving one of his poems, I was usually quite ill for several days.

She stated that when Poe's spirit finally appeared to her,

he was full of majesty and strength, self-poised and calm, and it would seem by the expression of his countenance, radiant with victory, that the reward promised to "him that overcometh" had been made his sure possession. Around his brow, as a spiritual emblem, was an olive-wreath whose leaves glowed like fire.

In the introduction to her collection of received poetry, Doten answered any skeptics who dared doubt her claims of spirit communication by citing the similarity that the *Springfield Republican*'s critic noted between her received poetry and that actually written by Poe:

By referring to the introductory remarks, copied from the "Springfield Republican," it will be seen that the supposition is presented, that I, or "the one who wrote the poem," must have been very familiar with the writings of Poe. Since no one wrote the poem for me, consequently I am the only one who can answer to the supposition.

Writing in support of Doten's claims in the introduction to an 1891 reprinting of "The Streets of Baltimore" in *Frank Leslie's Popular Monthly*, Clara Dargan Maclean compared the work favorably to Poe's authentic poetry:

The verses are indeed suggestive of their accredited author in their imagery, alliteration, onomatopoeia, and music of rhythm. To Poe's unique poem they may not unworthily stand as a complement. If the real author had any conception of its value, he (or she), might have given to the world a name worthy to be inscribed, in this instance at least, upon the page of fame beside that of the illustrious subject here so effectively impersonated.

One of James Carling's illustrations for Poe's poem "The Raven."

While Doten was falling under Poe's influence, the medium M.J. Wilcoxson also received poetry from Poe. In 1867, she published "The Midnight Prayer: An Inspirational Poem," a work reminiscent of "The Raven." Like Doten, Wilcoxson also claimed to see Poe's spirit. According to her preface, "An Intelligence purporting to be Poe has a number of times controlled my organism, both in the trance and the impressional state....In this superior state, I saw Poe, desponding, nervously excited, hurridly start for his boarding house, with a wild haggard look."

She found the poem popular enough to reprint in her 1872 book *The Vestal: A Collection of Articles in Prose and Poetry, Comprising a Short Essay on Origin and Destiny*, which was released on the twenty-fifth anniversary of the Fox sisters' first séance, which marked the birth of Spiritualism.

According to the Liverpool-born artist James Carling, Poe's spirit did not limit itself to composing poetry from beyond the grave. Around 1883, the young sidewalk artist and vaudeville performer set out to illustrate "The Raven" the way Poe would have intended. In the process, Carling boasted, "I have followed his meaning so close as to be merged into his individuality." Carling's niece, who sometimes posed for him, claimed that her uncle actually began to resemble the poet—transforming into him.

Like Poe, Carling died young and was buried in an unmarked grave. He did not live to see his "Raven" illustrations published. Fortunately, Carling's brother had the foresight to save the drawings, and they are now housed in the Poe Museum, where you can see for yourself if Poe could have had a hand in producing them.

Chapter 11

THE SÉANCE

While Sarah Helen Whitman was desperately trying to commune with her lost love, Poe's worst enemy was making his own attempts to contact the other side.

The spring air blew through the windows of Rufus Griswold's upper-floor library, the walls lined with thousands of books, including several of his own—popular anthologies of American and British writers, even a book of mourning poetry to comfort the grieving. A corner table's legs buckled under a pile of manuscript fragments and magazine clippings scribbled through with penciled corrections and notes, the materials he had gathered for the first posthumous collection of Poe's works.

Seated next to Griswold was Horace Greeley, editor of the *New-York Tribune*, the paper that, eight months earlier, had hired Griswold to write Poe's obituary. Griswold had taken advantage of the opportunity to trash the man he had envied and despised in life but had been too cowardly to do so while his target was still breathing. The obituary began by matter-of-factly reporting that "Edgar Allan Poe is dead," before adding that, although "this announcement will startle many…few will be grieved by it." The reverend went on to praise Poe's writing while suggesting that he was a drunken scoundrel doomed to wander the streets at night, mumbling curses on humanity. Griswold would continue his hatchet job and seal Poe's posthumous reputation with the biographical sketch to be included in the *Works of Edgar Allan Poe*, on which he was presently engaged.

Rufus W. Griswold from an 1845 engraving by G. Parker after a painting by J.B. Read.

Next to Greeley sat Dr. Marcy, Dr. Hawks, Dr. Francis, John Bigelow, Richard Kimball, Henry Tuckerman and General Lyman. They were joined by literary lions including Poe's friend and defender Nathaniel Parker Willis, novelist James Fenimore Cooper, poet William Cullen Bryant and the *Tribune*'s contributor George Ripley, whose report of the night's activities in the June 8, 1850 issue provided the details for this chapter. While most of those who accepted Griswold's invitation were avowed skeptics, Greeley, still reeling from the death of his son, was determined to make contact with the other side. He found hope in the news out of Hydesville that the Fox sisters could communicate with spirits at will. He had brought the girls and their mother to his Manhattan mansion, where he could prepare them to share their message with a wider audience. They would soon spread the new Spiritualist religion around the globe. Tonight's demonstration before New York's leading writers was just the beginning.

Across the library from the half-circle of chairs, the Fox sisters, Leah, Kate and Maggie, sat on a sofa behind a small table. Their watchful mother, Margaret Fox, hovered nearby. At the sisters' direction, Griswold pulled the shutters, closing out the teeming metropolis. Another guest extinguished the coal oil lamps, plunging the room into shadow.

The nonbelievers squirmed in their chairs for what seemed like an eternity. Greeley strained to hear even the slightest sounds in the darkness. There was the chatter of friends on the street, the scratch of a mouse inside the wall and other indistinct noises that might or might not be a spirit. But whose ghost could it be? Poe's and Griswold's friend Frances Osgood had succumbed to tuberculosis just a few weeks earlier, so Griswold, who kept a cherished painting of her hanging next to Poe's portrait in his hallway, likely wanted to hear from her. Other guests were anxious to contact their own deceased friends or relatives. Given how many of the guests had known him and how recently he had died, more than a few of them must have hoped to receive a message from Poe. But the silence continued.

Someone must have sighed in boredom because the sisters instructed the guests to pull their chairs closer to the table. Once the shuffling and grumbling subsided, the group heard the faintest of taps from under the floor. Ever so slightly louder, the next one seemed to emanate from the table. The one after that might have come from somewhere else within or without the library. Even though nobody was sure where the raps were coming from, the sounds were definitely getting more distinct and frequent until they refused to be ignored. Everyone could hear them, but the skeptics still wanted proof that this was a paranormal manifestation and not a party trick. Marcy put the phenomenon to the test by asking the first question. He was answered by a series of knocks, which the sisters translated for him. A few others tried to quiz the spirits, but the sisters' translations of the knocks proved unsatisfactory.

Cooper asked a few questions, but the answers, as decoded by the sisters, were insufficient. He then said, "Is the person I inquire about a relative?"

They heard more knocks, which the sisters told him had answered in the affirmative.

Then he asked how long ago this person had died.

A rapid succession of raps filled the air while the guests struggled to count them. By the time the tapping stopped, nobody could agree on how many knocks there had been. One thought there were forty-eight. Another believed it was fifty-four. Cooper asked the sisters to request that the spirit repeat the knocks a little more slowly. The spirit obliged. The total was fifty, and Cooper verified that his sister had, indeed, died fifty years earlier.

Then he asked if she had died by being struck by lightning, by drowning or by being thrown from a horse. The spirit knocked to the last one, which was correct.

Rising from their sofa, the sisters glided in unison to the center of the room. Even as they stood there, a knock came from a distant door. Accompanied by their host, the girls retired to the parlor directly underneath the library while a few skeptics stayed upstairs to search the room for evidence of trickery. The knocking resumed. It was coming from the empty couch on which the sisters had been sitting. When the men approached it, the sofa trembled.

Despite all the unexplained activity, the evening's séance produced few converts. In his *Tribune* article on the event, George Ripley wrote that he left with "a discreet, and somewhat apathetic noncommittalism."

Griswold opined in the July 22, 1850 issue of the *International Weekly Miscellany*, "We certainly could never for a moment be tempted to a suspicion that there is anything supernatural in the matter. Such an idea is simply ridiculous and will…be tolerated only by the ignorant, feeble-minded, or insane."

Eveleth apparently mistakenly believed Griswold was a believer when he wrote the latter on September 7, 1852:

> *Perhaps, too, Mr. Poe's spirit might be interested in its perusal—be so kind as to communicate it through Mrs. Fish, or some other one of the "Mediums[.]" By the way I sent a few words of comment upon some of*

the points of Eureka, *to Mr Poe by Mrs Whitman—that is I sent the words to her, with the request that she would forward them by the spirit Telegraph.*

Despite his skepticism, the recently separated (but not yet legally divorced because he feared the bad publicity it might bring) thirty-five-year-old Griswold became a fan of thirteen-year-old Kate Fox and borrowed her album for so long that one of her friends felt the need to write, asking him to return it.

Chapter 12

THE HAUNTED PEN

The tombstones were silhouetted against the crimson sky, and the burying ground was thrown into shadow. The grave diggers had just enough daylight left to make out the ground directly in front of them, but even that was quickly fading. Their shovels were searching for something solid, but they were already five feet down and running out of time.

The autumn wind nipping his bald dome and ears, the old sexton, George Spence, stroked his beard as he leaned on a nearby stone. It had been twenty-six years since he buried Poe, and he was certain this was the spot. How could he forget? He had been bringing curious tourists there since the beginning. After a while, he placed a little sandstone block over Poe's grave, just in case somebody needed to find it when he was not there.

The only other marker was the tangle of weeds. One of Poe's New York admirers offered to bring Poe's remains there and give them a suitable monument, but after falling out with Poe's mother-in-law, she abandoned the plan. A few years after that, over a decade after Poe's death, his cousin Neilson paid for an Italian marble headstone for Poe. A stonecutter carved "Hic/ Tandem Filicis/Conduntur Reliquae/EDGAR ALLAN POE/Obiit Oct. vii./1849" ("Here, at last, he is happy. Edgar Allan Poe, died Oct. 7, 1849") across the front and "Jam parce sepulto" ("Spare these remains") on the back. It would have been a fine memorial to the poet, if only a train had not jumped its tracks and crashed through the shop, shattering the stone.

An early photograph of the monument placed on Poe's second grave in 1875.

Fifteen years later, Poe was finally about to get a marker. The problem was that he was in such a remote corner of the lot that any monument would be practically hidden from the street. If Poe were to have a marker worthy of him, it would have to be in a place of honor, where passersby could not help but see it from the sidewalk. That meant Poe needed to be moved, and, as the man who had buried him, Spence was the one who could be absolutely certain where he was. Spence led the grave diggers, reporters and dignitaries to the spot that chilly afternoon. But hours later, they were starting to have their doubts. Could Poe's body have been stolen the night after his burial by one of the local medical schools and ended up on a student's dissecting table?

Then one of the shovels struck something solid. Spence rose and walked over to the pit. The smell of damp clay filled his nostrils. Pointing a lantern downward, he saw they had hit a rock. Somebody scooped it up and tossed it onto a pile of other stones.

The *Sun*'s reporter shot a glance at the one from the *Evening News*, wondering if it was time to call it a day. Then the shovel hit something solid, but this time it was soft. It was wood. The diggers scrambled to uncover the board. Then another. Then a coffin lid.

Spence, his assistants and the reporters gathered around the hole while a professional coffin mover named W.L. Tuder directed the operation. The diggers found the edges of the casket and cleared enough dirt to get underneath it.

At Tuder's order, they strained to pull the mahogany box out of its hole. As the top of the coffin reached the lip of the pit, the lantern light revealed it was still together. The witnesses closed in to see it rise. All dead silent, they waited in reverence for the whole coffin to reach the surface. The man from the *Sun* stepped forward, held his breath and leaned into the artifact.

A jarring thud threw him backward as the wood shattered at his feet. Placing his hand over his chest, he returned to the coffin, where Spence and the others were shining their lights across the bleached bones, glowing against the deep brown wood. The legs were intact. The hips and vertebrae were still in place, but the ribs had fallen to either side. Only a few loose fibers remained of his clothing.

Then there was the skull with that distinctive broad, sloping forehead that nobody who had known the living poet could fail to recognize. One of his critics thought it looked like a snake's. Others thought it indicated a genius. Phrenologists had studied the shape of that head, determining that it showed prominence in the regions of idealism while the temples displayed evidence of a certain nervousness of temperament.

The mandible had fallen off but retained all of its pearly teeth. Although the teeth from the maxilla had dislodged and scattered, three of the reporters wrote the next day about how white and perfect they were.

Spencer grabbed the remnant of the poet's face and gazed deep into its empty sockets. Yes, this was the man he had buried. A hardened clump of something, maybe dirt or maybe a calcified tumor, rattled around inside before he dropped it into the new box.

Whatever else was left of Poe and most of his casket were piled into a container about two and a half feet long. At sunup, they would be buried in the new plot, and later that day, readers of the *Sun*, the *Evening News* and the *Baltimore American* would read all the lurid details of Poe's unexpected appearance. (The part about the skull was recounted by Spence himself in the February 26, 1893 issue of the *New York Times*.)

Before leaving, the reporters snatched a few chunks of Poe's old coffin as souvenirs. At least a couple are preserved just as they were found that evening. One is in Baltimore's Enoch Pratt Free Library, while the other ended up in Richmond's Poe Museum. Several of the others were made into penholders, one of which is in the Pratt, while another found its way into a private collection. Journalist May Garrettson Evans also owned one.

Yet another one of the pens reached the actor and playwright George Hazelton. The pen's first owner, whose husband was one of the reporters who snatched a piece of coffin during Poe's move, took her fragment to a carpenter to have it carved and polished under her constant supervision (because she feared he would steal her coffin fragment for himself and carve her pen out of some worthless wood). Then she hired a jeweler to craft the ornate silver nib.

Some thirty-three years later, she met the forty-year-old actor in Baltimore. With years of performing under his belt, his first attempt at writing a play was *The Raven: The Love Story of Edgar Allan Poe*. A moderate success, it would eventually be adapted into a silent film. As a dear old friend of the actor, she must have known of his interest in Poe and thought this slightly morbid relic just might inspire Hazelton's forthcoming novel about the poet's life.

Hazelton reluctantly accepted the gift—not because he put any faith in the supernatural or the Spiritualism craze but because this pen just *felt* uncomfortable. Maybe it was the weight or the texture of the ornately carved wood rubbing against his fingers, but his hand recoiled from the touch of it. Or was it the knowledge that this had lain alongside Poe's decaying remains all those years?

What happened next was recorded in an interview with Hazelton from the April 10, 1909 issue of the *Cincinnati Inquirer*. According to the author, late one night he placed a few sheets of blank paper on his writing desk as he always did and began his novel, as would be expected, by writing "Chapter 1" at the top of the first page. To his annoyance, he saw the word "Eronel" written over his words. One of his children or servants must have gotten into his paper.

He pulled out a fresh page, inspected it to ensure there was nothing written on it and jotted "Chapter" only to see "Eronel" appear in its place. Rubbing his eyes, he wondered if this had also previously been written on the sheet. Maybe his pen had run dry. If this were the case, whatever he thought he was writing would not appear on the page, but the word "Eronel," which was apparently already on the paper, showed up instead. In this way, he had, if only for an instant, allowed him to trick himself into thinking that the word "Chapter" had somehow transformed into "Eronel," a word that, incidentally, didn't mean anything to him. He wasn't even sure what language it was. Maybe German?

The mystery solved, he dipped his pen into his inkwell, well supplied with fresh black ink, but when he tried to write the next line, the pen spurted a thick crimson liquid all over his white shirt. No matter how hard Hazelton forced the pen tip onto the page and struggled to draw absolutely anything else, the fragment of Poe's coffin refused to write anything but "Eronel." At length, he admitted defeat and abandoned all hope of using that cursed pen. As if the object were somehow pleased by this, the bloodstains immediately faded away.

Hazelton could not keep such a story to himself. It wasn't long before several of his friends dropped by to inspect the two sheets. While most tried to offer reasonable explanations or to translate the mysterious word, one of them came up with the idea of placing a mirror next to the inscription to reveal that it read "Lenore" backward.

With the help of a more agreeable writing instrument, Hazelton managed to finish his book. *The Raven: The Love Story of Edgar Allan Poe* appeared in 1909, and six years later, his Poe biopic, also called *The Raven* and based on his play of the same name, hit theaters. It is not hard to imagine that he invented the above story to drum up publicity for his novel. The location of his Poe coffin pen is unknown, and it is not certain if it is—or is not—either the one in the Pratt or the one in a private collection.

Chapter 13

THE RAVEN RETURNS

To say that William Fearing Gill was a Poe fan would be an understatement. Not only did he write articles and a book on Poe's life, but he also recited Poe's poetry on stage for the unveiling of Poe's Monument at the Westminster burying grounds. This was after Poe's remains had been relocated twice and placed into a second, hopefully more durable, container. Gill later purchased Poe's old cottage in the Bronx. Any of those things could qualify him as a Poe fan, but he took it a step further.

According to Gill, he was visiting a small cemetery in Fordham, New York, around 1875. After all his research, he could not have helped knowing that Poe himself had frequented this very place. There was one grave in particular that Poe visited day after day, throwing himself onto the earth and weeping uncontrollably. It was this spot that inspired him to write the couplet

Deep in earth my love is lying
And I must weep alone.

Maybe the poem was too personal, too painful, to complete. He wrote only those two verses and nothing more on the back of a manuscript for "Eulalie," his poem celebrating the joys of married life.

That marriage had ended in a tiny cottage in the woods of Fordham where his wife succumbed to tuberculosis. Always short of funds, he relied on the charity of friends and admirers to provide medicine and care for her,

A postmortem portrait of Poe's wife, Virginia, painted in 1847.

but when that proved insufficient to protect her from the biting chill of winter nights, he covered her in his old great coat and placed his loyal tortoiseshell cat on her chest to keep her warm.

When Virginia finally breathed her last, her nurse provided a burial shroud, and his landlord made room for her remains in his family crypt. At least that is the official story. If she were in a crypt, why would Poe have written about her being buried in the earth?

A quarter century later, Gill was wandering through that neglected old country cemetery when he approached the spot. The crunch of shovels greeted him. When he asked one of the grave diggers what was happening, they informed him they were relocating all the graves to make way for new construction. One of the men shoveled a pile of dry bones toward Gill's feet, informing him that these unclaimed remains were about to be discarded.

Grabbing one of the pieces, Gill inspected it. This delicate, slender bone could only be hers. This was the spot. He knew it well. Confident that this was all that remained of Poe's beloved Virginia, Gill took all that he could scoop into a small box and carried it home, where he kept it in the first place you would think to store the bones of a famous poet's muse—under his bed. He hid them under there for years, occasionally inviting guests to caress the remains of Annabel Lee, the real-life inspiration for Poe's poem of the same name.

In a December 30, 1899 *New York Evening Post* article titled "The Bones of Annabel Lee," the author, identifying himself only as "J.P.M.," recounted that callers to Gill's house could see the "few, thin, discolored bones," the ownership of which Gill seemed eerily proud.

According to Gill's account, he was sleeping over the bones, as peacefully as one could under those circumstances, when a raven flew into his window, alighted on his bed and issued an ominous croak. Whether it was real or a dream, Gill saw this as a message from his hero that it was time to give up the bones.

Contacting Poe's Baltimore relatives, Gill arranged to have the box of bones taken to the Westminster Burying Grounds to be buried next to her husband.

So was Gill contacted by Poe's angry spirit? A better question would be, whose bones were those under his bed? Even if we accept that Virginia Poe was buried in the ground (as Poe's poem suggests) and not in his landlord's crypt (as the landlord's family maintains), we would also have to believe that Gill arrived at Virginia's grave at exactly the right moment to save her remains. Stranger things have happened in the world of Poe.

Chapter 14

THE COLLECTOR

D r. Robertson held up the letter for closer inspection. He had been scanning the shelves of London's most distinguished antiquarian bookstore until his eyes hurt. Although not really looking for anything in particular, somehow he knew he had just found it.

Brushing the mop of white hair out of his eyes, he read the opening lines while scratching his bushy mustache. In his wrinkled gray suit and scuffed shoes, one might be surprised to learn that he was the founder and director of the Livermore Hydropathic Sanitarium, a facility devoted to the treatment of mental illness. Though he had established his mental hospital in California to take advantage of its mild climate, dry air and secluded location, Robertson had descended from an old Virginia family and still had ties to the East Coast, which he often visited to attend historical memorabilia auctions and to search for antiquarian books. Being a man of medicine and science did not prevent him from becoming a devout Spiritualist.

Spiritualism's popularity exploded in the early twentieth century. While the public had been drawn to the occult and mysticism for years, the previously inconceivable loss of life seen during the Great War drove millions to any medium who held out hope of hearing one last word from a deceased sibling, spouse or child. The number of lives lost both on the battlefield and at home is still staggering. Historians have trouble agreeing on the number, but it falls between six and twelve million, and that does not include the deaths caused by the Spanish flu pandemic that immediately followed the war.

John Robertson at the Poe Museum in 1933.

The Fox sisters, who confessed they had faked the knockings by cracking their toes (and later recanted that confession), were long gone. New generations of mediums outdid each other with increasingly elaborate claims of séances featuring furniture levitating, musical instruments playing on their own, ectoplasm streaming from mouths and other orifices, flower petals and food falling from the sky and more.

Traveling mediums would send advance scouts to upcoming venues in order to check the obituaries for information about the recently deceased. That way, the medium could "reveal" all manner of details to their grieving loved ones. Famed illusionist Harry Houdini had learned this trick during his own stint as a fraudulent medium. His experiences inspired him to search for an authentic medium to help him communicate with his mother's spirit, but every one he encountered turned out to be a fake. This, in turn, caused him to devote himself to tracking down and exposing fake mediums and their scams.

Almost overnight, Spiritualism descended from its peak of popularity to its nadir. But the truly devout continued to tout their evidence of spiritual contact. Among these apologists were the journalist William T. Stead, Arthur Conan Doyle and, to a smaller extent, John Wooster Robertson.

THAT BRINGS US TO the day in London when the bookseller at Southerin's Rare Books handed Robertson a letter he thought would be of interest. It was a note to Edgar Allan Poe from a Scottish Spiritualist convinced that Poe's account of the mesmerism of a dead man must be true. The psychiatrist was intrigued. Could the famous poet have been a devotee of the movement?

Having never heard of this article, "Mesmerism in Articulo Mortis," Robertson decided to investigate. He consulted the London-based bibliophile and book hunter James Tregaskis, who just happened to have a copy of the pamphlet, which, as you read in a previous chapter, is a British bootleg reprinting of Poe's purely fictional "The Facts in the Case of M. Valdemar."

Upon leafing through the flimsy pages, Robertson had a revelation and was inspired to collect the first printing of everything Poe ever wrote. This was only the first step in Robertson's quest to understand the workings of Poe's mind. The results of his research were the books *Edgar Allan Poe: A Psychopathic Study* and *Edgar Allan Poe: A Bibliographic Study*. These were combined to form *Poe: A Study*. Robertson intended these to present a new vision of Poe as a mystic and clairvoyant.

In *A Psychopathic Study*, Robertson proposed that Poe could only have written the way he did through the use of a "sixth sense" accessed through "auto-hypnosis." This trance state is similar to that Andrew Jackson Davis or the twentieth-century healer Edgar Cayce entered into in order to receive visions and communicate with spirits. Poe, Robertson believed, must have possessed personal knowledge of auto-hypnotism because he so accurately described it in the tale "Berenice," in which the narrator enters a trance by focusing a little too intently on his wife's teeth.

Of this sixth sense, Robertson wrote:

> *No subject of recent years has excited more interest among psychologists than this question of a "sixth sense." Although eminent names recently have added to those who acknowledge definite belief in spiritualistic phenomena, no answer can be made that may be considered final; nor has any proof been adduced that this "sixth sense," which I believe does exist, is more of a phenomenon than the other five, except that only highly organized "sensitives," or mediums, possess it.*

In the same essay, Robertson cited Sarah Helen Whitman's accounts as evidence that Poe possessed a "mesmeric power" he unconsciously used to control others. In this sense, Poe could be regarded as a powerful clairvoyant alongside Swedenborg, Davis and Cayce.

Robertson was so thoroughly convinced that his new interpretation of Poe's life and works would change the way we see the author that he donated his Poe collection to the Poe Museum in Richmond in order to ensure it would stay together and remain accessible to students. While his gift did form the core of the newly founded museum's collection, it also coincided with the waning of Spiritualism's popularity.

So many fake mediums had been exposed by Houdini and others that *Scientific American* offered a reward for anyone who could provide evidence of the paranormal. Some might have tried, but nobody was able to claim the prize. Robertson's beliefs had been discredited, and his reinterpretation of Poe was disregarded and forgotten.

A decade later, when Gabriel Wells published the 1934 article "Poe the Mystic" in the *American Book Collector,* he assured his readers that "none of the table-rapping or ghost conjuring manipulation is intended." On the contrary, Wells viewed Poe's mysticism, as expressed in *Eureka,* as akin to that of Einstein or Lemaître, who might have seemed incomprehensible mystics in the early twentieth century but are recognized as trailblazing scientists or cosmologists today. While in Poe's time his stories concerning animal magnetism were deemed thoroughly realistic and scientific, they are now considered pseudoscience and magic. Conversely, *Eureka* appeared mystical and pantheistic at the time of its publication, but with the passage of time, some of his strangest ideas have come to be accepted as forerunners of modern cosmology. Poe has even been given credit for solving Olbers' Paradox, or the question of why the sky is dark at night.

Decades would pass before the late twentieth century's revival of interest in paranormal investigations. By the twenty-first, this would amount to a boom. Both amateur and professional ghost hunters, armed with the latest recording and detection equipment, flocked to old houses, abandoned asylums and spooky castles around the globe in search of that ever-elusive evidence that spirits walk among the living. It was only a matter of time before they followed in Sarah Helen Whitman's footsteps and came calling for Poe's ghost.

part iii

POE'S
HAUNTS

In death—no! even in the grave all is not lost.
Else there is no immortality for man.

—Edgar Allan Poe, "The Pit and the Pendulum"

Chapter 15

POE'S GHOSTS

A blood-curdling shriek pierced the air. All heads turned to the door, through which bolted a young girl pursued by a tiny, enshrouded specter.

They circled the card table occupied by the leading members of Richmond society. In addition to the young Poe's foster father, John Allan, there were Allan's business partner Charles Ellis, Philip Thornton of Rappahannock and the celebrated War of 1812 veteran General Winfield Scott, "Old Fuss and Feathers" himself. The gentlemen had gathered for an evening of cards and brandy, only to have the whole thing thrown into disarray by Ellis's young daughter and her phantom pursuer.

But the ghost met his match in the old general, who leapt over the spilled drinks and scattered cards to stop the intruder. The specter stopped in his tracks and turned to find himself cornered. When the general lunged for him, the ghost dodged and bounded for the door—only to get whacked across the head by Scott's walking stick.

Scott grabbed the intruder, ripping off its shroud to reveal little Edgar Poe underneath.

This just might be the earliest sighting of Poe's ghost, even if it was just a prank. His disembodied spirit has been turning up all over the place ever since. During Poe's forty-year life, he spent time in Richmond, New York, Philadelphia, Boston, Baltimore, Charleston, London, Providence and Charlottesville. Poe was born in Boston and began his military career there. Richmond was the city he called home. He spent most of his childhood and began his career in journalism there. He returned at the end of his life to renew his engagement with his former childhood sweetheart. New York is the city where Poe published "The Raven" and saw the height of his fame. He retreated from the city to a small cottage in what is now the Bronx. As you may recall, this is where Poe's wife died. He was still renting the cottage two years later at the time of his death but had been traveling for the last three months of his life. Poe died in Baltimore. In his early twenties, he published his first short stories while living there. He had little to do with the city until decades later, while passing through the city, he died in Washington College Hospital under mysterious circumstances.

Even though Poe lived in a number of different homes in each of these cities, his surviving residences are remarkably few. None of his houses survives in Richmond (where he spent more of his life than any other city), Boston or Manhattan. Only one of his Philadelphia homes, one of his Baltimore homes and his cottage in the Bronx survive. His dorm room at the University of Virginia remains, although historians are not sure whether it was actually #13 West Range, which is the officially recognized Poe Room today.

Fortunately, sightings of Poe's ghost are not limited to his homes. Legend has it that his restless spirit has turned up everywhere from city sidewalks to barstools. What follows are a few stories from the poet's favorite haunts.

Chapter 16

POE IN BALTIMORE

he Charm City was the home of Poe's father, the troubled actor David Poe Jr., who probably died before Edgar turned three (although history does not record the precise time or location of his death, which took place after he abandoned his wife and children).

More importantly, Baltimore was home to several other Poe relatives who actually did play important roles in his life. His grandfather "General" David Poe Sr. served as the honorary quartermaster general of Baltimore during the Revolutionary War, earning the appreciation and friendship of no less a figure than the Marquis de Lafayette. During an 1824 visit to the city, Lafayette called on David's widow, Elizabeth Poe, and urged the United States government to provide her with a pension in honor of her late husband's service to Lafayette and the Continental army. This meager $247 per year virtually ensured that her poorest relatives would flock to her home for support. By the time Edgar Poe moved to Baltimore in 1831, a penniless University of Virginia dropout who had recently been expelled from West Point, he had no prospects for employment and would have ended up on the streets if not for Elizabeth Poe.

By this time, her row house on Wilks Street was crammed full of relatives, including her widowed daughter (and Edgar's aunt) Maria Poe Clemm, Clemm's children Henry and Virginia and Edgar's brother, Henry. How the family managed to scrape together enough to support itself is unknown, but Edgar devoted himself to writing, selling his works to magazines and entering literary contests. While he watched his older brother lose his battles

Poe's home in Baltimore.

with tuberculosis and the bottle at the age of twenty-four, Edgar might have even worked as a bricklayer—maybe finding the inspiration for stories like "The Black Cat" and "The Cask of Amontillado," which both feature the hiding of bodies behind walls.

A couple years later, the family (now without Poe's brother) moved to slightly better lodgings on Amity Street, in the building that is now the Edgar Allan Poe House and Museum of Baltimore. Edgar Poe would stay there until 1835, when he moved to Richmond. It was not long before he lost both his grandmother and his cousin Henry, so Poe moved the last two members of the household, Maria Clemm and her daughter Virginia, to Richmond with him.

Several tenants occupied the cramped row house over the next century. While the Baltimore Poe knew fell around it, the house survived as a reminder of the desperate early days of his career, when he wrote to survive. Each story sold or contest won provided just enough money to keep food on the table another day. It was in this house that Poe wrote his first horror story and first science fiction tale. It was also there that he met and grew dependent on his future wife, Virginia. She was only nine years old when they first met, and at that time, he used her to carry love letters to his lady friends.

By 1941, this literary landmark was scheduled for demolition. At the urging of some concerned citizens, the city agreed to spare the house if someone could determine which of the row houses on the block was Poe's. Journalist May Garrettson Evans, who also happened to be a member of the Poe Society of Baltimore, set to work scouring old maps and records to find any evidence of the house's correct address while taking into account that the numbers on the individual buildings had changed over time. She was able to identify the correct house in time to rescue it from the wrecking ball. The Poe Society managed the site for decades before the City of Baltimore's Commission for Historical and Architectural Preservation took it over. In 2012, the city, in turn, handed off the management to a private foundation.

Poe Baltimore now operates the house as a museum where visitors can explore the rooms in which Poe wrote some of his early masterpieces. These claustrophobic spaces and narrow staircases have been known to make visitors uneasy. In fact, horror film legend Vincent Price once stated, "This place gives me the creeps." So it seems only fitting that the building would be haunted.

According to L.B. Taylor's *Ghosts of Virginia, Volume III*, on November 10, 1979, the psychic John Krysko investigated Poe's garret room, where the sloping roof makes standing up straight possible only in the center of the floor. Krysko reported feeling "loneliness" at the site and claimed to sense Poe having spirited conversations with an unidentified friend or business associate who was trying to help Poe get some of his early works published. Krysko also reported, "The spirit of Edgar Allan Poe tells me that he wanders the house looking for a yet-unfound manuscript."

A "night security officer" at the house told Krysko of seeing a flickering light moving from room to room at night, as if someone were carrying a candle. A similar flickering light was witnessed in the house during the 1968 Baltimore riots, when the neighborhood was without electrical power. A neighbor at the time called the police, but no source for the mysterious glow could be found.

The September 18, 1999 issue of the *Baltimore Sun* records the impressions the Poe House had on the neighbors, some of whom thought Poe's spirit runs across the rooftops of nearby homes, terrorizing the neighborhood and torturing children. None of these children has, however, stepped forward to tell of their encounters with Poe, who, in life, actually liked children. In August 1999, a local man claimed to have looked into the window to see a shadowy figure sitting at a writing desk.

A member of the Poe Society told me that a psychic had informed him of glancing up from the sidewalk to see a mustached man sitting at a writing desk in the garret, writing "The Raven." The level-headed Poe expert informed him that the window is at such an angle that one would not be able to see a man sitting at a writing desk in that room, that Poe did not grow a mustache until a decade after he moved out of the house and that he did not even start writing "The Raven" until several years later. I might also add that not everyone is convinced that the garret was even his room. Virginia might have stayed up there while Edgar lived on a lower floor.

A former curator of the house, Jeff Jerome, told of an incident that took place while an actor was changing in an upstairs bedroom for a performance. Jerome was downstairs when he heard a thunderous crash and rushed upstairs to investigate. Pressed back against a far wall, the actor pointed to a window frame that had lifted up and out of its groove to fly across the room, as if someone had tossed it at him. Throwing his costume at Jerome, the frazzled actor told him, "I don't get paid enough for this," as he hurried down the stairs. Ever since, people visiting that room have reported feeling watched.

Despite all the reports of ghostly activity, it was not until thirty years later, in 2012, that Jerome finally allowed a group to conduct a paranormal investigation in the house. Using a combination of electrical equipment and old-fashioned divining rods, Ghost Detectives conducted the search during a dark May night. Their video documentation has since been posted online. They spent a lot of time sitting in dark rooms, asking Poe questions about his life and cause of death, but there was no evidence that he answered.

After his 1979 visit to the Poe House, John Krysko headed to Poe's final resting place at the nearby Westminster Burying Grounds, where he reportedly felt pulled by Poe's spirit into the catacombs and "guided by an invisible force" to Poe's original grave (which is not in the catacombs). The cemetery being fairly small and Poe's original grave well marked and centrally located, it would not be difficult to find Poe's grave even without the assistance of an "invisible force."

Nearby, the building in which Poe died is still standing. At the time of his death, it was Washington University Hospital, but it has gone through several different owners over the centuries before coming into the possession of Johns Hopkins University, which plans to use it as housing or an assisted living facility. The building is not open to the public.

Naturally, there are accounts of his spirit appearing in the building, even though the room in which he breathed his last has since become part of a stairwell.

Vague accounts also tell of a black-clad spirit resembling Poe drunkenly stumbling down the Baltimore sidewalks he once roamed. Maybe he is on his way to the home where he first lived with his cousin and future wife, Virginia. Alternatively, he could be reliving the hazy last days that ended with his discovery, semiconscious at Ryan's Fourth Ward polls. History has not recorded exactly what he was doing during the preceding few days in Baltimore, but many speculate he was on a bender.

Some say he still is. The Horse You Came in On, which claims to be the last tavern Poe visited before his death, blames the unexplained rattling of a chandelier on the poet. Just in case he returns, the Fells Point bar even reserves a seat for him. Legend has it (and some regulars will vouch for the story) that patrons who deny the presence of his ghost will have their stools pulled out from under them.

Chapter 17

POE IN AND AROUND
PHILADELPHIA

A couple hours' drive north in Philadelphia, Poe lived for six years and wrote most of his best fiction, including "The Tell-Tale Heart," "The Black Cat" and "The Fall of the House of Usher." Although he lived in different homes around the city, only one of these has survived, and it is now administered by the National Park Service. Compared to Poe's surviving residences in Baltimore and the Bronx, this one is more spacious and, in Poe's time, would have been situated on the rural outskirts of town. This is where Poe enjoyed a brief period of prosperity before he was forced to move to New York in search of new prospects. Today, however, the house is empty. Bare plaster walls are all that remain of the place Poe would have known. The furniture and artwork are long gone, but visitors can still imagine the presence of the poet and his family in those vacant halls. Maybe it is more than just imagination. Vague, anonymous accounts circulating online (where everything *must* be true) tell of sightings of Poe's ghost wandering about the house to this day.

There are also reported Poe appearances at places Poe only briefly or allegedly visited. One such place is Philadelphia's Fairmount Waterworks adjacent to the site of the reservoir into which John Sartain claimed a manic Poe nearly threw himself in the summer of 1849. In his book *Philadelphia Ghost Stories*, Charles J. Adams III recounted that a "well respected trance medium" believed Poe's energy is trapped in "a spiral of spiritual energy" in the Fairmount Waterworks and that a "researcher" spoke of a troubled, confused spirit appearing to visitors on the walkway between the Philadelphia Museum of Art and the Waterworks.

In nearby Merion, Pennsylvania's General Wayne Inn, where Poe supposedly carved his initials onto a windowsill in 1843, the poet's spirit is said to be seen drinking at a favorite table. His presence is also reported just south of Philadelphia at the Deer Park Inn and Tavern in Wilmington, Delaware. According to legend, Poe visited the inn once and had such a bad time he issued the curse, "May all who are born here die here, and may all who come here never leave." Since people have been known to cross Wilmington's city limits without dying, that hex may not have been entirely effective. Regardless, some of the unidentified noises heard at the tavern are blamed on Poe's spirit.

Chapter 18

POE IN THE BRONX

A lthough Poe's Manhattan homes have all been lost to time and the wrecking ball, his spirit is said to be seen at no fewer than six different locations there, one of which was not even built until half a century after his death. But just across the Harlem River in the Bronx, one of Poe's homes still stands.

When Poe lived in the area, it was fourteen miles outside New York City. What is today the Bronx was countryside with rolling hills and cherry trees. Poe moved there in hopes that the fresh air would cure his wife's tuberculosis. Today, the house stands across the street from its original location and is maintained and interpreted by the Bronx County Historical Society. Between Poe's own rocking chair and the actual bed in which his wife breathed her last, the place can give a visitor the feeling that the Poes have just stepped outside for a walk and might step back through the front door at any moment. It is no wonder people might expect to see the writer's ghost there, rocking in his favorite chair.

On April 13, 1980, Stephen Kaplan and his wife, executives with the Parapsychology Institute of America, went to Poe's cottage in the Bronx and may have captured Poe on camera for the first time since 1849. Kaplan was a radio personality and author who is best known today for his vocal skepticism of the "Amityville Horror" hauntings. While investigating the Poe Cottage, they photographed a "light mist" floating around Poe's rocking chair. Weeks later, the mist in the photograph appeared to have more distinct form. The next week, the mist seemed to the Kaplans to

Poe's rocking chair from a 1920 photograph taken in his Fordham cottage by Charles W. Stoughton.

resemble Poe sitting in his chair. They even thought he seemed to have a hint of a smile on his face. In his book *True Tales of the Unknown*, Kaplan reported, "Poe's spirit remains with the living; he is eternally rocking in a rocking chair, not only in a cottage in the Bronx, New York, but also in a carefully guarded photograph."

I have yet to see the photograph and cannot verify the appearance of the mist or the conditions under which the photograph was taken.

Chapter *19*

POE IN PROVIDENCE

The few nights Poe spent in Providence sent him careening from the heights of his engagement to the depths of his suicide attempt. Many of the pivotal moments during this time took place in or near the Providence Athenaeum, a member-supported private library. It was within this columned Neoclassical temple of learning that Poe and Sarah Helen Whitman sneaked away to read poetry between the bookshelves. He even signed his name underneath the poem "Ulalume" in one of the bound volumes.

Sarah Helen Whitman's
house in Providence.

One might expect to find Poe's and Whitman's spirits drifting hand in hand through the stacks, but I have not found such an account. Instead, Poe is said to spend his time roaming the top floor and occasionally awakening lone patrons who begin to doze off while reading. A slightly less romantic yarn is recorded by Julie Tremaine and Tony Pacitti in a September 13, 2017 post on Providenceonline.com. They recount that long after Poe's death, an unnamed witness came across a man sleeping on the front steps. When asked to move, the sleeping or drunken man shouted, "The Conqueror Worm!" before vanishing.

Could it have been Poe's ghost, or was it the spirit of a poetry-loving vagrant?

Not far from the Athenaeum, locals claim sporadic late-night sightings of a man in black, wearing a top hat and carrying a walking stick as he makes his way down Benefit Street near Whitman's house. According to *Haunted Providence: Strange Tales from the Smallest State* by Rory Raven, those who have told the tale recognized him as none other than Edgar Allan Poe.

Chapter 20

POE AT FORT MONROE

The plausibility of any of these anonymous, unverified accounts is highly suspect, but the sheer volume of Poe sightings in Virginia strains credulity. At Fort Monroe, near Hampton, Poe ended his army enlistment in 1829, but he returned twenty years later to stay at the old Hygeia Hotel, where he gave a reading of "Ulalume" one moonlit summer night with the waves lapping the shore behind him. The hotel may have been demolished, but the old casemate still stands just as it did when Poe was an army artificer. Although not very tall, it is a suitably imposing structure with thick stone walls surrounded by a moat. The interior is dark and claustrophobic. The structure might be a museum these days, but it still retains the kind of ominous atmosphere that might have inspired the twenty-year-old poet. The museum's mannequin of Edgar Allan Poe at his writing desk seems right at home there. But this is not where Poe's specter is said to appear.

According to L.B. Taylor's *Ghosts of Tidewater*, an unnamed family living on the base in the late 1960s claimed to see him multiple times. They were living in quarters that backed up to Ghost Alley. (Somehow, on a base already crammed full of wandering spirits, this spot is especially haunted.) One night in May 1968, a woman residing in the house heard a gentle rapping from the first floor. When she went downstairs to discover the source, she encountered a man in the shadows, wearing antiquated clothing with puffy sleeves. From what she could discern of his features

Fort Monroe in 1884.

through the darkness, she thought he bore a striking resemblance to Edgar Allan Poe. This Poe—or Poe lookalike—seemed to sneer at her before dematerializing through a window.

The following year, the tenant saw him again. This time, the Poe-like figure staggered down the hallway in a "bent-over, crouching" position before he disappeared through a closed door.

Chapter 21

POE'S BRIDE IN PETERSBURG

Several miles inland, at the Hiram Haines House in Petersburg, where Poe is said to have spent his honeymoon, locals say that his wife can be spotted peering out of one of the upstairs windows on her wedding anniversary.

A former owner of the house, Jeffrey Abugel, author of *Edgar Allan Poe in Petersburg*, purchased the structure after it had fallen into disrepair from years of use as a used office furniture store. In the process of restoring the building and recovering its lost history, he identified the room in which Poe likely spent his honeymoon. There Abugel found some original mantels and paint. With these pieces still in place, it was easy to imagine how the room would have looked in Poe's day, so Abugel brought in a bed frame and embellished the walls with a painting to complete the look.

Just like Rufus Griswold and Sarah Helen Whitman before him, Abugel held his own midnight séances in that chamber in hopes of communicating with the long-lost poet. They might not have heard from Poe, but they say there are plenty of other spirits in residence, possibly including Virginia Poe.

Chapter 22

POE AND FRIENDS IN RICHMOND

A half hour's drive north, in Richmond, the garden in which Poe used to sneak away to see his sweetheart Elmira Royster is now occupied by the Linden Row Inn. While only a small fraction of the garden remains, the hotel, which occupies a series of row houses built between 1847 and 1853, does conjure up a Poe-esque atmosphere with photographs of the author and a Poe-themed suite.

With all the references to Edgar and Elmira throughout the hotel, one would expect to encounter their spirits reliving one of their youthful excursions in the courtyard, but this is not the case. Rather, it is Poe's mother whom people claim to see. In an article titled "Ghostly Shades of Poe at Linden Row in Richmond," in the November 13, 2010 issue of the *Washington Post*, Zofia Smardz reported that a relative told her Poe's mother haunts the grounds because she died in one of the buildings. This rumor continues to circulate even though none of the buildings on the block existed during her lifetime. It is also known that she died about seven blocks east of Linden Row. Just how the story got started is anyone's guess.

There might be another Poe sighting a couple miles west of the inn at Talavera, where Poe read "The Raven" for Susan Talley and her family a couple weeks before his death. In Poe's time, it was a modest farmhouse in the countryside west of Richmond, but that all changed with the outbreak of the Civil War. After the Talleys fled, the army cleared the land and demolished the outbuildings. Only the house survived, and it was in the middle of fortified earthworks called Battery 10.

Susan Talley returned to live in the desolate landscape. What once held orchards, vineyards and greenhouses was now wasteland littered with dismantled gun carriages and rusty bayonets scattered about the tall grass. She moved out in the 1870s, and the place went through a series of owners. While much of the house was updated and expanded in the early twentieth century, the old mantel by which Poe stood while reciting "The Raven" was retained.

Over the years, the surrounding countryside was filled with early twentieth-century row houses, and Talavera was divided up into apartments. Decades of neglect took their toll on the old farmhouse until a group of historic preservations bought it in 1975 and began restoring it. One of the members was Poe enthusiast Sergei Troubetzkoy, who purchased the house in 1983. Like any true Poe fan, he supported the Poe Museum, helping clean its model of Richmond and offering to drive one of the museum's VIP visitors to the airport in Washington. The dignitary just happened to be Vincent Price, who had recently starred in his seventh cinematic adaptation of Poe's works. At Troubetzkoy's invitation, Price came to Talavera, where, standing next to the original mantel, he recited some lines from "The Raven" on the very spot where Poe once stood.

When interviewed by L.B. Taylor in 1985 for *Ghosts of Richmond*, Troubetzkoy revealed, "A lot of people who have lived here believe the house to be haunted." Specifically, he mentioned a male ghost who made himself known to several tenants. One recounted that for several nights in a row, someone climbed into bed with him. Others claimed to feel cold spots in the middle of summer.

Troubetzkoy recalled feeling a presence over him while he was painting his apartment one day. It is the sort of thing you get used to while living in a haunted house. Just then, two of his friends happened to walk past his open door and told him they saw a man standing behind him. Although Troubetzkoy never saw this specter, he told Taylor, "We'd like to think he's the ghost of Poe."

Poe was also said to make appearances at the old Allan house Moldavia. According to Mary Wingfield Scott, whose grandfather rented the place in the 1880s, after the Allans had moved out, children would still point out the very door on top of which sat the "pallid bust of Pallas" on which the raven perched in Poe's most famous poem. As young girls, Scott's mother and sister trembled beneath their covers whenever they heard Poe's ghost descending the staircase, but she later confessed that it might have been mice.

A photograph of the Allan mansion Moldavia taken in 1890.

By far the least plausible account of a sighting of Poe's ghost is recorded in L.B. Taylor's *Ghosts of Virginia, Volume III*. According to the story, when a tour guide at Richmond's Poe Museum opened the front door to admit a guest, the visitor claimed to see Poe's ghost standing behind the guide and ran screaming down the street.

The Poe Museum houses the world's largest collection of Poe's possessions, including his clothing, walking stick, trunk, bed, chair and a lock of his hair taken after his death. Building materials salvaged from buildings associated with Poe include the staircase from one of his boyhood homes, which is installed in the museum's Elizabeth Arnold Poe Memorial Building, and the bricks from Poe's office, which have been made into a shrine in the museum's Enchanted Garden.

Given the concentration of artifacts from Poe's life preserved in the museum, it is tempting to think his spirit still lingers over some of these objects. In an article on Dreadcentral.com dated June 1, 2009, Sifu Scott reports:

> *The identity of the...apparition* [at the Poe Museum in Richmond] *cannot be positively named, but many who work at the museum and visit feel certain they know exactly who it is and why he is there. Often seen as a shadowy figure, it is believed that the restless ghost of Edgar Allan*

Poe himself visits the halls, attached to some of the items displayed in the museum. He is believed to be particularly attached to a hand mirror that once belonged to his beloved young wife, Virginia, as well as his walking stick which he left in Richmond a mere two weeks before his death.

After all the years I have worked at the museum, the first time I heard about this "shadowy figure" was when I read that article.

In the late twentieth and early twenty-first centuries, the investigation of the paranormal gained the aid of the latest audio and video recording technologies while retaining the use of mediums who carry on the tradition of Andrew Jackson Davis and the Fox sisters. One such medium, Patrick Matthews, visited the Poe Museum three times between 2006 and 2011, claiming each time to make contact with the spirits of Poe; his mother, Eliza Poe; and his wife, Virginia Poe. Matthews's team brought audio and video recording devices but captured no evidence of Poe's ghost in either of these media.

One of the Poe Museum's galleries in 1928.

The Poe Museum has also hosted several amateur paranormal investigators, but none has claimed to record a trace of Poe's ghost during its searches of the museum's buildings and garden. They have, however, reported that they believe several other unrelated entities are present in the museum complex. Many of these, incidentally, are said to be the ghosts of young children.

While some of the museum's guests tell me that Poe's presence can still be felt in the garden or that his powerful emotions have been deposited on the artifacts he once owned, the closest thing to a *sighting* of Poe's ghost at the Poe Museum might just be the story of a tour guide who, upon opening the gift shop one morning, found that the store's souvenir Poe bobbleheads had all left their shelves during the night to line up like toy soldiers on the floor. I suspect the guide's co-worker was to blame.

Chapter 23

ANNABEL LEE IN CHARLESTON

During his military service, Poe was stationed from 1827 until 1828 at Fort Moultrie on Sullivan's Island, near Charleston, South Carolina. The Lowcountry landscape must have made quite an impression on him because thirteen years later, he recalled it well enough to use it as the setting for his treasure hunt mystery "The Gold-Bug."

Poe also took advantage of his free time to visit Charleston, where he is said to have consulted the library for notices of his mother's performances on that city's stages. Charleston would become the setting for his tales "The Oblong Box" and "The Balloon Hoax."

The ghost story related to Poe might be the only one I have found in which a fictional character from one of his works has been spotted. According to legend, while Poe was stationed at Fort Moultrie, he fell in love with a local lady named Annabel Lee Ravenel. Because her father objected to his daughter seeing a lowly soldier, the two lovers sneaked away to the most romantic, scenic and secluded place they could find. You might have guessed this was a cemetery.

Behind the weathered brick walls of the Unitarian church graveyard, they met to profess their undying devotion and to plan their future. But it was not to be. He was transferred to Fort Monroe, and in his absence, she succumbed to yellow fever. When Poe supposedly returned to visit her grave, in the very cemetery where they used to meet, her father would not reveal its location, nor would he place a marker over her. It is said he even disturbed the soil over six different graves in order to confuse Poe.

The story goes that this inspired Poe, after the passage of two decades, to compose the poem "Annabel Lee." Traces of this legend might be suggested by the lines:

It was many and many a year ago,
  In a kingdom by the sea,
That a maiden there lived whom you may know
  By the name of Annabel Lee;—
And this maiden she lived with no other thought
  Than to love and be loved by me.

She was a child and I was a child,
  In this kingdom by the sea,
But we loved with a love that was more than love—
  I and my Annabel Lee—
With a love that the wingéd seraphs of Heaven
  Coveted her and me.

And this was the reason that, long ago,
  In this kingdom by the sea,
A wind blew out of a cloud by night
  Chilling my Annabel Lee;
So that her high-born kinsmen came
  And bore her away from me,
To shut her up, in a sepulchre
  In this kingdom by the sea.

The angels, not half so happy in Heaven,
  Went envying her and me:—
Yes! that was the reason (as all men know,
  In this kingdom by the sea)
That the wind came out of the cloud, chilling
  And killing my Annabel Lee.

But our love it was stronger by far than the love
  Of those who were older than we—
Of many far wiser than we—
  And neither the angels in Heaven above
Nor the demons down under the sea

Can ever dissever my soul from the soul
Of the beautiful Annabel Lee:——

For the moon never beams without bringing me dreams
Of the beautiful Annabel Lee;
And the stars never rise but I see the bright eyes
Of the beautiful Annabel Lee;
And so, all the night-tide, I lie down by the side
Of my darling, my darling, my life and my bride
In her sepulchre there by the sea——
In her tomb by the side of the sea.

The poem certainly depicts the sea, the grave and even her "high-born" family keeping them apart. If Annabel Lee really did inspire him to write the poem of the same name, this did not stop him from telling a few other women that they were the "real" Annabel Lee. Several others, including Stella Lewis and Sarah Helen Whitman, also claimed the poem was written about them. But some Charlestonians insist that their Annabel Lee is the right one, whether or not she ever actually existed.

Visitors to the old Unitarian church cemetery say one can still see Annabel Lee's ghost searching the tombstones at night to find her lost love. For a while, ghost tours would enter the site after dark to try to spot her, but the church has since grown so tired of the attention that it has banned nighttime visitors—except for possibly her.

Regrettably, there is no evidence to support the story, and Poe is not known to have mentioned it to anyone, even though it is exactly the kind of tale he would have told Sarah Helen Whitman during their strolls through the Swan Point Cemetery.

Poe did, however, know a Ravenel during his time at Fort Moultrie. Edmund Ravenel was a conchologist who kept a house on Sullivan's Island and may have been a model for the character Legrand, an eccentric entomologist living in near seclusion on that island, in "The Gold-Bug."

Poe, incidentally, also wrote a book about conchology, the study of shells. It turned out to be his bestseller during his lifetime.

Chapter 24

POE STILL SPEAKS
FROM BEYOND THE GRAVE

I n addition to those seeking to make contact with Poe's spirit in places in which he lived or that hold his possessions, there are some who still attempt to reach him through a traditional séance, much as Sarah Helen Whitman and Rufus Griswold did in the middle of the nineteenth century. In 2010, Peter Fenton, blogger and organizer of the Million Ghost March, claimed to have communicated with Poe's spirit at a séance. According to Fenton, Poe's message from beyond the grave was that Fenton should start the Edgar Allan Poe Community College, an online college for all things weird. Fenton considered it a "paranormal trade school."

According to one theory, Poe's spirit has already done more than launching a college—he has established his own religion. In 2013, Chaz Van Heyden published *The Reincarnation of Edgar Allan Poe*, in which he proposed a theory that Poe was the reincarnation of Benjamin Franklin. Poe, in turn, was reincarnated as the author L. Ron Hubbard, the founder of Scientology.

Poe might also be fighting crime. In her 2014 book *Forevermore: Guided in Spirit by Edgar Allan Poe*, Michigan psychic medium and author Kristy Robinett recounts how Poe became her spirit guide when she was thirteen and has been with her ever since. As an adult, Robinett uses her psychic abilities—and a bit of Poe's guidance—to consult law enforcement and private investigators around the United States in order to help find missing persons and close cold cases. She finds Poe's ghost very different from his popular reputation as a macabre and melancholy misanthrope. Rather, she finds him "an insightful guide and sleuth" who is "far from mad."

In life, Poe both invented the detective story and attempted to solve the real-life murder of New York cigar girl Mary Cecelia Rogers, and in death, according to Robinett, he continues to help unravel mysteries. Incidentally, Robinett has her own Investigation Discovery Network television program, *Restless Souls*, so that makes Poe her (albeit invisible) co-star. What other nineteenth-century author can say that?

CONCLUSION

P oe has certainly had a busy afterlife. According to the preceding accounts, he is searching for a manuscript in Baltimore; drinking at taverns in Baltimore, Philadelphia and Wilmington; wandering the streets of Baltimore and Providence; prowling a private library in Providence; visiting a museum in Richmond; glaring at people in Fort Monroe; and relaxing in his rocking chair in the Bronx. Could he really haunt so many places simultaneously?

An alternate, and far more mundane, explanation is a few cases of mistaken identity. Although many can instantly recognize Poe from a photo or drawing, the Poe Museum still receives several emails a year from people who have uncovered daguerreotypes or tintypes of dark-haired men with mustaches. Some of them bear only the slightest resemblance to Poe. (One of them turned out to be John Wilkes Booth.) It might be reasonable to assume that, if someone were to see a ghost of a dark-haired mustached man in appropriate attire, they might misidentify it.

Of course, there are many other possible explanations for these phenomena, ranging from optical illusions to rattling pipes, but it has not been my intention to prove or disprove any of them. As Stuart Chase put it, "For those who believe, no proof is necessary. For those who don't believe, no proof is possible." Even if there is not a shred of truth to any of these stories, they are still valuable as reflections of Poe's posthumous reputation. Taking them as a group, we can find a few common themes.

One of these motifs is the association of Poe with alcohol. Three of the preceding stories feature him drinking in taverns, and at least two others have him staggering, as if inebriated. During his life, Poe struggled with drinking because even a single glass of wine could make him drunk. For this reason, he went for long stretches without touching anything stronger than water. Unfortunately, Griswold's biography of Poe and Thomas Dunn English's writings about him helped popularize the idea that Poe lived in a constant state of intoxication. This became the popular opinion of Poe. Even though Griswold and English were trying to condemn or ridicule Poe's intemperance, today's public tends to enjoy this image of Poe as a modern, debaucherous rock star. This might explain why so many of the ghost stories connected with him depict him as either drinking or drunk. If someone owns a bar that Poe might have visited, it seems only fitting that they attribute any unusual activity to Poe's spirit rather than to that of some deceased regular or former bartender who might seem more likely to stick around after death.

Other legends portray Poe's ghost as a boogeyman who frightens children in Baltimore or in his since-demolished childhood home in Richmond. It seems only fitting that the master of terror would return to give everyone a fright. After all, the young Poe dressed up like a ghost to frighten Mary Ellis and enjoyed chasing her with a toy snake until she cried. As an adult, he is said to have been delighted by children following him down the street crying, "Nevermore! Nevermore!" to which he might jump out at them from around a corner with his arms flapping, sending the kids fleeing in all directions. Even his last reading of "The Raven" at Talavera was designed to thrill and delight his audience. One would expect Poe's ghost to share the same love of a good-natured thrill, even if it only manifests itself in spooking a drowsy reader at the Providence Athenaeum. But would the real Poe devote his afterlife to frightening people when only a small portion of his works were in the horror genre? His comedies outnumbered his terror tales, and those who knew him best describe him as being witty and good-natured—a far cry from the Poe myth perpetuated by Griswold.

Another motif appears to be that of Poe's ghost searching for something, whether it be a missing manuscript in Baltimore or some unidentified destination to which he walks on the streets of Providence, Baltimore or Fort Monroe. It appears that he has some unfinished business. Maybe his sudden death at the age of forty denied the world some great works that were yet to be written. He was, after all, at the height of his powers, with his instant classics "Annabel Lee" and "The Bells" first appearing in print just after his death, and he was in the middle of writing "The Lighthouse," which he left unfinished. A common feature of ghost lore is that of unfinished business, so these accounts fit perfectly into this tradition.

Of course, Poe's ghost is also said to be writing. Whether he is dictating his poems to a medium or sitting at his writing desk, Poe is said to continue to do what he did best. Whereas some other ghosts run headless through the towers where they were executed or continue to fight battles that ended two hundred years ago, Poe's spirit is content to sit down at his desk and write. It might not be as exciting as one of his horror tales, but it seems more appropriate.

Another notable feature of these stories is that Poe's spiritual manifestations are connected to multiple places, even ones he visited only briefly or not at all. Maybe this reflects Poe's image as a wanderer who never lived in any one house for more than a few years—and sometimes for only a couple of months. Although he called Richmond his home, he lived in Philadelphia, New York, Baltimore, Boston, London and other cities. He traveled to find work. He traveled to give lectures. He traveled to find love. Maybe he was never entirely at home anywhere. Poe's spirit, then, continues to move from place to place.

Whether or not there is any truth behind these tales, I am certain that Poe still speaks to us from beyond the grave. It does not matter if you find yourself in one of his old haunts—or anywhere else in the world. You can hear Poe's words and communicate with him simply by reading his works. Wherever and whenever his works are read, he is there. Just turn down the lights and enjoy one of his terror tales by candlelight. You will have no need for his ghost to appear to give you a good scare.

BIBLIOGRAPHY

Abugel, Jeffrey. *Edgar Allan Poe's Petersburg: The Untold Story of the Raven in the Cockade City*. Charleston, SC: The History Press, 2013.

Adams, Charles J. *Philadelphia Ghost Stories: Chilling True Stories of Haunted Places in the Most Historic City in America*. Reading, PA: Exeter House Books, 1998.

Allen, Hervey. *Israfel: The Life and Times of Edgar Allan Poe*. New York: George H. Doren, 1926.

Barden, Thomas E., ed. *Virginia Folk Legends*. Charlottesville: University of Virginia Press, 1991.

Barnes, Eric Wollencott. *The Lady of Fashion: The Life and Career of Anna Cora Mowatt*. New York: Charles Scribner's Sons, 1954.

Berman, Scott, and Sandi Berman. *Haunted Richmond: The Shadows of Shockoe*. Charleston, SC: The History Press, 2007.

Brill, Robert D. *The Mystery of "Mar'se Eddie" in the Shire: A Biography of Edgar Allan Poe's Scottish Connections*. Foster City, CA: Robert Densmore Brill, 2013.

Conan Doyle, Arthur. *The History of Spiritualism*. London: Cassell and Company, 1926.

Davis, Andrew Jackson. *Answers to Ever-Recurring Questions from the People: A Sequel to the Penetralia*. New York: J.S. Brown and Co., 1862.

———. *Events in the Life of a Seer: Being Memoranda of Authentic Facts in Magnetism, Clairvoyance, Spiritualism*. New York: J.S. Brown and Co., 1887.

———. *The Magic Staff: An Autobiography of Andrew Jackson Davis*. New York: J.S. Brown and Co., 1857.

Fisher, Benjamin F., ed. *Masques, Mysteries, and Mastodons: A Poe Miscellany*. Baltimore: Edgar Allan Poe Society of Baltimore, 2006.

Harrison, James A. *The Life and Letters of Edgar Allan Poe*. New York: T.Y. Crowell, 1902.

Mabbott, Thomas Ollive. *The Collected Works of Edgar Allan Poe*. Vols. 1–3. Cambridge, MA: Belknap Press of Harvard University Press, 1969 and 1979.

McNeil, W.K., ed. *Ghost Stories from the American South*. Little Rock, AR: August House, Inc., 1985.

Neale, Gay. *Brunswick County, Virginia: 1720–1975*. Lawrenceville, VA: Edmonds Printing, 2000.

Ostram, John Ward, Burton Pollin and Jeffrey Savoye. *The Collected Letters of Edgar Allan Poe*. 3rd ed. New York: Gordian Press, 2008.

Raven, Rory. *Haunted Providence: Strange Tales from the Smallest State*. Charleston, SC: The History Press, 2008.

Robertson, John Wooster. *Edgar A. Poe: A Study*. San Francisco: Bruce Brough, 1921.

Robinett, Kristy. *Forevermore: Guided by the Spirit of Edgar Allan Poe*. Woodbury, MN: Llewellyn Publications, 2014.

Scott, Mary Wingfield. *Houses of Old Richmond*. New York: Bonanza Books, 1951.

Semtner, Christopher P. *Edgar Allan Poe's Richmond: The Raven in the River City*. Charleston, SC: The History Press, 2012.

———. *The Poe Shrine: Building the World's Finest Edgar Allan Poe Collection*. Charleston, SC: Fonthill Media, 2017.

———. *The Raven Illustrations of James Carling: Poe's Classic in Vivid View*. Charleston, SC: The History Press, 2015.

Silverman, Kenneth. *Edgar Allan Poe: A Mournful and Never-Ending Remembrance*. New York: Harper Perennial, 1992.

Taylor, L.B. *The Ghosts of Richmond*. Lynchburg, VA: Progress Printing Company, 1985.

———. *The Ghosts of Tidewater*. Lynchburg, VA: Progress Printing Company, 1990.

———. *The Ghosts of Virginia*. Vol. 3. Lynchburg, VA: Progress Printing Company, 1996.

Thomas, Dwight, and David K. Jackson. *The Poe Log: A Documentary Life of Edgar Allan Poe, 1809–1849*. Boston: G.K. Hall and Co., 1987.

Troubetzkoy, Sergei. *Talavera* (booklet). Printed by author, 1986.

Van Heyden, Chaz. *The Reincarnation of Edgar Allan Poe*. Nashville, TN: Velvet Gloves Publishing, 2013.

Weiss, Susan Archer. *The Home Life of Poe.* New York: Broadway Publishing Company, 1907.

Wells, Gabriel. *Poe the Mystic.* Metuchen, NJ: Gabriel Wells, 1934.

Whitman, Sarah Helen. *Edgar Poe and His Critics.* New York: Rudd & Carleton, 1860.

Wilcoxson, M.J. *The Vestal: A Collection of Articles in Prose and Poetry, Comprising a Short Essay on Origin and Destiny.* Chicago: Religio-Philosophical Publishing House, 1872.

INDEX

ABOUT THE AUTHOR

Visual artist and curator of the Edgar Allan Poe Museum, Christopher P. Semtner has curated and designed critically acclaimed exhibits for museums and galleries across the country. Semtner has also written several books and chapters on topics including Poe, visual art and crime fiction, in addition to contributing articles to Biography.com, *Crime Writers' Chronicle* and other publications. He has been interviewed for BBC4, PBS and NPR and featured in publications including the *New York Times* and Forbes.com. He regularly speaks about strange and macabre subjects at various venues from the Steampunk World's Fair to the Library of Congress and as far away as Japan.

Visit us at
www.historypress.com